Plato's Dialogue on Friendship

An Interpretation of the *Lysis*, with a New Translation

Plato's Dialogue on Friendship

An Interpretation of the *Lysis,* with a New Translation

DAVID BOLOTIN

CORNELL UNIVERSITY PRESS
ITHACA AND LONDON

Cornell University Press gratefully acknowledges a grant from the Andrew W. Mellon Foundation that aided in bringing this book to publication.

First published 1979 by Cornell University Press.
Published in the United Kingdom by Cornell University Press Ltd., 2-4 Brook Street, London W1Y 1AA.

International Standard Book Number 0-8014-1227-7
Library of Congress Catalog Card Number 79-4041

Printed in the United States of America

Librarians: Library of Congress cataloging information appears on the last page of the book.

To my wife

Contents

Introduction

If we wish to find philosophic discussions of friendship, we
are almost compelled to turn to the writings of classical antiq-
uity. The question of friendship was an important one for ancient thinkers. Yet in modern times, philosophers have rarely
given it an explicit place in their moral teaching or in their
treatment of social and political life. Friendship does not seem
to fit into any of the modern systems of thought. Our individ-
ualism, for example, must distrust or disregard the natural so-
ciety among friends. There is no room for the generosity of
true friendship in those doctrines which begin from the
premise that man is naturally selfish. And at the other pole of
modern thought, our hopes for universal, or even national,
brotherhood tend to make us lose sight of so private and ex-
clusive a relationship. Friendship is too natural to figure prom-
inently in teachings which deny that man's freedom to perfect
his social and political life is limited by his nature.

Whatever the reasons, however, for the decline of friendship as a theme in modern thought, its importance for our
lives is scarcely any less than it ever was. Men still agree with
Aristotle that friendlessness is something dreadful, and we appreciate Francis Bacon's view that without true friends "the
world is but a wilderness." More particularly, we are still
aware of the close connection between friendship and philosophy itself. In Socrates we have the model of a philosopher

whose way of inquiry was through friendly conversation and whose love of friends was second only to his love of wisdom. And we too, or at least many of us, regard the pleasures of friendship as among the deepest and surest rewards of the life of learning. With a view, then, to a better understanding of the philosophic life as well as of our own lives, it is useful to return to the ancient discussions of friendship.

The traditional subtitle of Plato's *Lysis* is "On Friendship." The *Lysis* is the only surviving work by a classical Greek author which is devoted entirely to this theme. Yet it has received relatively scant attention from recent scholars.[1] This neglect seems to stem from the widespread belief that the dialogue is little more than a prelude to the fuller treatments of friendship (*philia*) and love (*erōs*) in the *Symposium* and in the *Phaedrus*. Now it is true, and apparent from the dramatic setting of the *Lysis,* that Plato sees a kinship between friendship—at least in some of its aspects—and erotic passion (*erōs*). Moreover, the *Lysis* does anticipate many of the features of the *Symposium* and the *Phaedrus.* Yet the fact remains that Plato chose to investigate friendship as a distinct theme in this separate dialogue. The *Lysis* is a complete work, which must be interpreted as a whole in its own right before it can be properly appreciated in the context of Plato's other writings. Accordingly, and in the belief that the *Lysis* could well be Plato's most revealing discussion of friendship, I have tried to understand it on its own.

The most immediate question raised in the *Lysis* can be

---

1. For a full bibliography, see Donald Levin, "Some Observations concerning Plato's *Lysis*," in *Studies in Ancient Greek Philosophy*, edited by John Anton with George Kustas (Albany, 1971), pp. 236–258. See also Gregory Vlastos, "The Individual as an Object of Love in Plato," *Platonic Studies* (Princeton, 1973), pp. 3–11, 35–37.

stated quite simply. It is the question of the relationship between friendship, on the one hand, and the wants and needs of
imperfect beings, on the other. Is there a friendly love which
is wholly free of need? That is to say, does all friendship depend upon the friends' deficiencies, or is there a higher type of
friendship that unites those who admire and cherish each other
simply because of one another's goodness?

From the dialogue, it would appear that Socrates both asserts and denies that there is this higher friendship. For he first
subscribes to an allegedly Homeric view that friendship exists
between likes, who—since the bad are unstable and not even
alike to themselves—turn out to be equivalent to the good.
Only those who are good, then, could be friends in the true
sense. Yet soon afterward Socrates challenges this claim by arguing that the good, as such, are self-sufficient and in want of
nothing. As a result, he says, they neither long for each other
nor need each other, and they are thus incapable of friendship.
Socrates' denial of the possibility of friendship between the
good prepares the way for a new suggestion of his own, namely that those who are neither good nor bad become friends of
the good. In other words, friendly love—in the best sense—is
the love of imperfect beings, like us, for those who are good
and capable of helping us to become better and happier. According to this suggestion, our friendly love of the good
depends on the presence of evils and on our need to free
ourselves from them. There is consequently no reason to
believe that the good would return the love which they
receive. The generosity, as well as the reciprocity, we associate
with friendship is missing from this account. Socrates himself
thus rejects this second thesis and asserts that there could still
be friendship even if all evils were eradicated. Accordingly, he
returns to the previous claim that friendship unites the good

with each other. But then, recalling his apparent refutation of that thesis, he abandons the argument and leaves us in confusion. We are left to wonder about a perfect friendship, independent of wants and needs, which seems not to exist, and an imperfect one, admittedly depending on need, which fails to account for the whole phenomenon of friendship.

The dialogue seems to offer no resolution of this perplexity and no answer to Socrates' question "What is a friend?" Instead, it encourages us to seek clarity on our own. Yet considerable guidance toward this end is available within the dialogue, if only it is read with sufficient care. Excellent discussions of how to read a Platonic dialogue have been published by Leo Strauss and by Jacob Klein,[2] and so here I will mention only one key point. The reader himself must become involved in the dialogue and concerned to learn the truth about the matters it discusses. In particular, whenever an argument or an assertion by Socrates, though satisfying to his interlocutors, fails to convince us, we must not hesitate to interject our own questions. If we refrain from this questioning, we implicitly assume that Socrates is wrong and that we are wiser about the matter at issue than he. And yet many of our objections could stem from unacknowledged ignorance on our own part. Or, as is also possible, Socrates' argument may be intentionally faulty or his assertion intentionally false. Plato's dialogues, as we know, are dramas rather than treatises. And his Socrates, who is known for his irony, may have good reasons for making some false claim or for using some faulty argument with a view to a particular interlocutor. Now Plato did not, of course, want to conceal his thought from the

2. Leo Strauss, *The City and Man* (Chicago, 1964), pp. 50–63. Jacob Klein, *A Commentary on Plato's "Meno"* (Chapel Hill, 1965), pp. 3–31.

readers for whom he wrote.[3] It may well turn out, then, if our questions or objections are simple and clearly stated, that the dialogue addresses them somewhere. Our own questions to Socrates can even lead us toward the heart of the dialogue. Indeed, the dialogue is like an able teacher, a teacher who has more to say to us the more willing we show ourselves to learn. Only after opening ourselves to the possibility of such learning can we hope to ascertain what the dialogue really means, or what Plato really thought. And this knowledge, which is the goal of an interpreter, is a prerequisite for judging wisely whether, or to what extent, his thought is true.

My commentary on the *Lysis* is accompanied by a new and literal translation. I have translated primarily with a view to those who wish to study the dialogue with care. In order to place as few barriers as possible between Plato and such readers, I have aimed at word-for-word accuracy, a goal which I regard as second in importance only to the need for intelligible English. There frequently are small variations between the rendering of a passage in the translation, on the one hand, and in the commentary, on the other. These discrepancies arise because I made some concessions in the commentary toward a more natural English style. Though in my judgment all these concessions are unimportant, I might of course be mistaken about some of them, and therefore I could not allow them in the translation itself. My translation is based upon the Oxford Classical Text, *Platonis Opera,* III (Oxford, 1903), edited by John Burnet. All deviations from the readings of that edition are indicated in the footnotes to the translation.

I have also included as an appendix an essay devoted to a scholarly controversy, which focused on the *Lysis,* between

3. See *Republic* 450d10–451a4.

Max Pohlenz and Hans von Arnim. Though this controversy took place between 1913 and 1921, it still offers the most illuminating analysis of the dialogue that I have found. My discussion of this dispute is placed after the commentary because it presupposes considerable familiarity with the *Lysis*. For classicists, however, and others already acquainted with the dialogue, this essay might be read more profitably as a further introduction to the commentary.

A Translation of
Plato's *Lysis*

203a   *Socrates:* I was on my way from the Academy straight to the Lyceum,[1] along the road outside the wall and close under the wall itself. When I came to the little gate near the spring of Panops,[2] I happened to meet there Hippothales, son of Hieronymus, Ctesippus of Paeania,[3] and with them other youths, standing together as a group. And Hippothales, seeing me approaching, said, "Socrates, where are you on your

b   way to and where from?"

"From the Academy," I said, "I'm on my way straight to the Lyceum."

"Come here then," he said, "straight to us. Won't you stop in? It's worth it,[4] you know."

"Where do you mean?" I said. "And who are you all?"

"Here," he said, showing me a kind of enclosure set against the wall and with a door opened. "We ourselves," he said, "pass our time here, along with a great many others—good-looking ones,[5] too."

204a   "And what is this here? And what is your pastime?"

"It's a palaestra,"[6] he said, "built recently. And for the most part we pass our time with speeches,[7] which we would be pleased to share with you."

"That's a fine thing to do," I said. "And who teaches here?"

"Your companion," he said, "and praiser—Miccus."[8]

17

"By Zeus," I said, "the man is not an inferior one, but a capable[9] sophist."

"Do you wish to follow us, then," he said, "so that you may see those who are there?"

b   "I would be pleased to hear, first, what terms I'm to enter on and who the good-looking one is."

"Each of us," he said, "has his own opinion about who he is, Socrates."

"But who is he in your opinion, Hippothales? Tell me that."

At this question he blushed. And I said, "Hippothales, son of Hieronymus, you no longer have to say whether you love[10] anyone or not. For I know not only that you love, but also that you are far along the way in love already. I am inferior

c   and useless in other things, but this has somehow been given to me from a god—to be able quickly to recognize both a lover and a beloved."

On hearing this, he blushed still much more. And then Ctesippus said, "How refined that you blush, Hippothales, and shrink from telling Socrates his name! And yet if he spends even a short time with you, he'll be tormented by hearing you speak it so frequently. Our ears, at any rate, Socrates,

d   he has deafened and has filled them full of Lysis. Indeed, if he drinks a little, it's easy for us to suppose—even when we wake up from sleep—that we hear the name of Lysis. And the descriptions he goes through when he's talking, though they're dreadful, are not quite so dreadful as when he tries to flood us with his poems and prose writings. And what's more dreadful than this is that he also sings about his favorite, in an astonishing voice, which we have to endure hearing. Yet now, when questioned by you, he blushes."

e   "Lysis is quite young," I said, "as it seems. I gather this because I didn't recognize his name when I heard it."

"That's because they don't often say his name," he said, "but he's still called by his father's,[11] because his father is so widely recognized. For I know well that you're far from ignorant of the boy's looks;[12] indeed, he's capable of being recognized just from that alone."

"Let it be said," I said, "whose [son] he is."

"He's the son of Democrates of Aexone,"[13] he said, "his eldest."

"Well, Hippothales," I said, "how noble[14] and dashing in every way is this love which you have discovered! But come now and display for me too the things you display for these fellows, so I may know whether you understand what a lover needs to say about his favorite to him or to others."

"Do you attach any weight, Socrates," he said, "to what this fellow has been saying?"

"Do you deny," I said, "even loving the one he speaks of?"

"No, I don't," he said. "But I do deny making poems about my favorite or writing prose."

"He's not healthy," said Ctesippus. "He's raving and he's mad."

And I said, "Hippothales, I'm not asking to hear any of your verses or any song you may have composed[15] about the youth. But I want the thought, so that I might know in what manner you approach your favorite."

"Surely this fellow will tell you," he said. "For he understands it and remembers precisely if, as he says, he's been talked deaf from always hearing me."

"By the gods," said Ctesippus, "very much so. In fact, it's ridiculous, Socrates. For how can it not be ridiculous that he—who's a lover and who has his mind on the boy more than the others do—has nothing private to say which even a boy couldn't tell? What the whole city sings about Democrates and the boy's grandfather Lysis, and about all his ancestors—their wealth, their horse-breeding, and their victories at the Pythian, Isthmian, and Nemean games with four-horse chariots and with riding-horses—these things he makes into poems and speaks about. And in addition, there are things still more antiquated than these. For just the other day he described for us, in a kind of poem, the entertainment of

d   Heracles. He told how their ancestor welcomed Heracles because of his family connection with Heracles—for the ancestor himself was a son of Zeus and of the daughter of their deme's[16] founder. This is the sort of thing that old women sing, Socrates, and there are many others like it. And he compels us to listen to him speaking and singing these things."

And when I heard this, I said, "Ridiculous Hippothales, are you composing and singing a song of praise about yourself before you've won the victory?"

"But it's not about myself, Socrates," he said, "that I compose or sing."

"You don't suppose so, at any rate," I said.

"Then how is it?" he said.

e   "These songs," I said, "are directed most of all toward you. For if you catch your favorite, and he's of this sort, then what you've said and sung will be an adornment to you and a real song of praise, just as if you had won a victory in obtaining such a favorite. But if he escapes you, the greater the praises you have spoken of your favorite, the greater will be

206a   the fine and good things you'll have been deprived of, and you'll be thought ridiculous. Therefore, whoever is wise in love-matters, my friend, does not praise his beloved before he catches him, since he fears how the future will turn out. And at the same time, those who are beautiful are filled full with proud thoughts and bragging whenever someone praises and exalts them. Or don't you suppose so?"

"I do," he said.

"And don't they become harder to capture, the greater braggarts they are?"

"That's likely, at least."

"And what sort of hunter, in your opinion, is someone who scares away his prey as he hunts, and makes it harder to capture?"

b   "Clearly an inferior one."

"And indeed, not to beguile but to make savage through speeches and songs—that's very unmusical. Isn't it?"

"Yes, in my opinion."

"See to it, then, Hippothales, that you don't make yourself liable to all these things because of your poetry. And indeed, I suppose you wouldn't be willing to agree that a man who harms himself through his poetry is ever a good poet; for he is harmful to himself."

"No, by Zeus, I wouldn't," he said. "For that would be c very unreasonable. But it's because of these things, Socrates, that I'm consulting with you. And if you have anything else, give your advice as to what to say in conversation or what to do so that someone might become endeared to his favorite."

"It's not easy to say," I said. "But if you were willing to make him enter into discussion with me, perhaps I might be able to display for you what you need to say to him in conversation instead of the things which these fellows assert that you say and sing."

"Well, that's not at all difficult," he said. "For if you enter with Ctesippus here and then sit down and converse, I suppose that he will come to you himself—for he is exceedingly d fond of listening, Socrates. Moreover, since they're observing the Hermaea,[17] the youths and the boys are mingled in the same place; so he'll come to you. And if not, he's well-acquainted with Ctesippus because of the latter's cousin, Menexenus. For he happens to be a closer companion to Menexenus than to anyone else. Let Ctesippus here call him, then, if it turns out that he doesn't come himself."

"That's what needs to be done," I said. And at the same
e   time I took Ctesippus and went into the palaestra. The others went after us. When we entered, we found that the boys had offered a sacrifice there and that what had to do with the victims was already nearly done. The boys were playing with knucklebones,[18] and all of them were dressed up. Now the majority were playing outside in the courtyard, but some were in the corner of the dressing room, playing at odd-and-even, with a great many knucklebones which they selected from some little baskets. There were others standing around them and looking on. Among the latter was Lysis. He was
207a   standing among the boys and youths, crowned with a wreath, and he stood out by his appearance as someone worth being spoken of not only for being beautiful, but because he was beautiful and good.[19] And we went over to the opposite side of the room and sat down—for it was quiet there—and we began some conservation with each other. Then Lysis started to turn around frequently to look at us. Evidently, he desired to come over. Now for a while he was perplexed, and he
b   shrank from coming over to us alone. But then Menexenus, in the middle of his playing, entered from the courtyard, and when he saw me and Ctesippus, he came to sit down beside us. On seeing him, Lysis then followed, and he sat down beside us along with Menexenus. Then the others also came toward us. And in particular Hippothales, when he saw rather

many of them standing near by, screened himself behind them and approached to where he supposed Lysis wouldn't see him, for he feared to incur his hatred. And in this way he stood near and listened.

And then I looked toward Menexenus and said, "Son of
c Demophon, which one of you is older?"

"We dispute about that," he said.

"Then there would also be strife," I said, "about which one is nobler."[20]

"Very much so," he said.

"And likewise, indeed, about which one is more beautiful."

Here they both laughed.[21]

"But I won't ask," I said, "which one of you is wealthier. For you [two] are friends, aren't you?"

"Very much so," they [both] said.

"Well the things of friends are said to be in common, so you [two] won't differ in this respect, if indeed you [two] are speaking the truth about your friendship."

They [both] assented.

d After that I was attempting to question them as to which one was juster and wiser. But in the middle of this, someone came up to fetch Menexenus, saying that the gymnastic master was calling him. It was my opinion that this was because he happened to be supervising the sacred rites. So then Menexenus had departed, and I began to question Lysis. "I suppose, Lysis," I said, "that your father and your mother love[22] you very much?"

"Very much so," he said.

"Then they'd wish for you to be as happy as possible?"

e "Well, how could they not?"

"And is a human being happy, in your opinion, if he were to be a slave and if it were not possible for him to do anything he desired?"

"No, by Zeus, not in my opinion," he said.

"Then if your father and your mother love you and desire that you become happy, it's entirely clear that they exert themselves so you should be happy."

"Well, how could they not?" he said.

"They allow you, therefore, to do what you wish, and they don't scold you at all, and they don't prevent[23] you from doing what you desire?"

"But by Zeus, they do indeed prevent me, Socrates, and in very many things."

"What do you mean?" I said. "While wishing for you to be blissful, they prevent you from doing what you wish? But tell me this. If you desire to ride in one of your father's chariots and to take the reins during a competition, would they not allow you, but prevent you instead?"

"By Zeus, no indeed," he said. "They wouldn't allow me."

"But then whom would they?"

"There's a charioteer, who is hired by my father."

"What do you mean? They entrust a hireling, rather than you, with permission to do whatever he wishes with the horses? And they also pay him for this very thing?"

"But of course," he said.

"But I suppose they entrust to you the rule over the team of mules, and if you should wish to take the whip and beat them, they would allow it."

"How would they allow it?" he said.

"What?" I said. "Is no one able to beat them?"

"But certainly," he said, "the muleteer."

"Is he a slave or free?"

"A slave," he said.

"Even a slave, it seems, they consider worth more than they do you their son, and they entrust their own things to him rather than to you, and they allow him to do what he wishes, but you they prevent. But tell me this further thing. Do they allow you yourself to rule over yourself? Or don't they entrust even this to you?"

"How would they entrust me with that?" he said.

"But who rules over you?"

"This one here," he said, "my attendant."[24]

"He's not a slave, is he?"

"But of course. He's ours," he said.

"It's dreadful indeed," I said, "that one who is free should be ruled by a slave. But also, what is it that this attendant does in ruling over you?"

"He attends me, of course, and leads me to school," he said.

"But these teachers, surely they don't rule over you?"

"Most certainly they do."

"That's a great many masters, then, and rulers whom your father voluntarily sets over you. But when you come home to your mother, does she allow you to do whatever you wish— so you may be blissful with her—either with the wool or with the loom, when she is weaving? For she doesn't prevent you, I suppose, from touching her flat blade, or her comb, or any other of her tools for spinning wool."

And he laughed and said, "By Zeus, Socrates, not only does she prevent me, but also I'd be beaten if I touched."

"By Heracles," I said, "surely you haven't done anything unjust to your father or your mother?"

"No by Zeus, not I," he said.

"But in response to what do they so dreadfully prevent you from being happy and from doing whatever you wish, and support you through the whole day always being a slave to someone and—in a word—doing almost nothing that you desire? So it seems that you gain no advantage from your possessions, great as they are, but everyone rules over them rather than you. Nor, it seems, do you gain any advantage from your body, which is so noble, but even this is shepherded and tended by another. But you rule over no one, Lysis, and you do nothing that you desire."

209a

"That's because I'm not yet of age, Socrates," he said.

"I doubt that this is what's preventing you, son of Democrates, since I suppose that there's this much which both your father and your mother do entrust to you and for which they don't wait until you're of age. For when they wish something to be read or to be written for themselves, you—I suppose—are the first one in the household whom they assign to this. Isn't that so?"

b

"Very much so," he said.

"In this, then, it's possible for you to write whichever letter you wish first and whichever one second. And it's possible to read in the same way. And, as I suppose, when you take up your lyre, neither your father nor your mother prevents you from tightening or loosening whichever string you wish, nor from plucking it with your fingers or striking it with the plectrum. Or do they prevent you?"

"Of course they don't."

c

"Whatever could be the cause, then, Lysis, for their not preventing you here, while in regard to the things we were speaking of just before, they do prevent you?"

"I suppose," he said, "it's because I understand these things, but not those."

"Very well," I said, "you best [of men]. So your father isn't waiting for you to become of age before entrusting everything to you, but as soon as he considers your thinking to be better than his own, on that day he will entrust both himself and his own things to you."

"That's what I suppose," he said.

"Well," I said, "but what about your neighbor? Doesn't he have the same standard concerning you as your father does?

d Do you suppose that he will entrust to you his own household to manage, as soon as he considers your thinking about household management to be better than his own? Or will he preside over it himself?"

"He'll entrust it to me, I suppose."

"And what about the Athenians? Don't you suppose they will entrust their affairs to you, as soon as they perceive that you think capably?"[25]

"I do."

"By Zeus," I said, "what then about the Great King? Would he entrust his eldest son—the one who is going to rule over

e Asia—with permission to throw whatever he wished into the sauce while the meat was boiling? Or would it be us rather, if we should come to him and give him a demonstration that our thinking about food preparation was finer than his son's?"

"Clearly he would entrust it to us," he said.

"And so he wouldn't allow him to throw in even a little. But he would allow us—though we grabbed salt by the handful—to throw it in if we wished."

"Well, how could he not?"

"And what if his son were diseased in his eyes? Would he

210a allow him to touch his own eyes—if he didn't consider him a doctor—or would he prevent him?"

"He would prevent him."

"But as for us—if he assumed that we were skilled in the medical art—even should we wish to open his eyes and sprinkle ashes inside them, I suppose he wouldn't prevent us, since he would consider our thinking to be correct."

"What you say is true."

"Then would he also entrust to us, rather than to himself or to his son, everything else in regard to which we are wiser, in his opinion, than they are?"

"Necessarily, Socrates," he said.

b   "This, then," I said, "is how it stands, my dear Lysis.[26] With regard to the things in which we become prudent, everyone—Greeks as well as barbarians, and both men and women—will entrust them to us; we will do in regard to these matters whatever we wish, and no one will voluntarily obstruct us. Rather, we ourselves shall be free in regard to them and rulers over others, and these things will be ours, for we shall profit from them. But with regard to those things in which we don't acquire good sense,[27] no one will entrust us with permission to do what is in our opinion best concerning

c   them; but everyone will obstruct us as much as is in his power—not merely aliens, but even our father and mother and whatever may be more closely akin[28] to us than they are. And we ourselves shall be subject to others in regard to those things, and they will be alien [property] to us, for we shall derive no profit from them. Do you grant that this is how it is?"

"I do grant it."

"Then will we be friends to anyone and will anyone love us in regard to those matters in which we're of no benefit?"

"Surely not," he said.

"Now, therefore, not even your father loves you, nor does anyone else love anyone else insofar as he is useless."

"It doesn't seem so," he said.

d   "Then if you become wise, my boy, all will be your friends and all akin to you—for you will be useful and good. But if you don't, no one else will be your friend, and neither will your father, nor your mother, nor your own kinsmen. Now is it possible, Lysis, for someone to think big in regard to those matters in which he's not yet thinking?"

"How could he?" he said.

"And if you require a teacher, you're not yet thought-ful."[29]

"That's true."

"Therefore, your thoughts are not [too] big, if indeed you're still thoughtless."

"No, by Zeus, Socrates, not in my opinion," he said.

e   And when I heard him I looked over toward Hippothales and almost committed a blunder. For it came over me to say, "This, Hippothales, is how one needs to converse with his favorite, by humbling him and drawing in his sails instead of puffing him up and spoiling him, as you do." But then I caught sight of him in agony and disturbed by what had been said, and I recalled that though he was standing near Lysis he wished to escape his notice. And thus I recovered myself and

211a held back from the speech. Menexenus, meanwhile, came back and sat down beside Lysis, which is where he had risen from. Then Lysis whispered to me very boyishly[30] and in a friendly way—unobserved by Menexenus—and he said, "Socrates, tell Menexenus too what you've been saying to me."

And I said, "You tell it to him yourself, Lysis. For assuredly you were applying your mind."

"Most certainly," he said.

b   "Try, then," I said, "to remember it as well as possible, so you can tell him everything clearly. And if you forget any of it, ask me again, when you first happen to come across me."

"Well, I'll do that, Socrates, most definitely so. You can be sure of that. But speak to him about something else, so I too may listen, until it's time to go home."

"Well, that's what needs to be done," I said, "since, indeed, you are bidding me. But see to it that you serve as my ally if Menexenus attempts to refute me. Or don't you know that he's contentious?"

"Yes, by Zeus," he said, "exceedingly so. And it is because of this, in fact, that I wish you to converse with him."

c

"So I may become ridiculous?" I said.

"No, by Zeus," he said, "but so you may chasten him."

"How so?" I said. "It's not easy, since he's terrifying[31]—that human being—he's a pupil of Ctesippus. And look, he himself is present—don't you see him?—Ctesippus."

"Don't be concerned about anyone, Socrates," he said. "But come on, converse with him."

"I must converse," I said.

Now while we were saying these things by ourselves, Ctesippus said, "Why are you [two] feasting alone by yourselves and not giving us a share of the speeches?"

d

"But we must share them," I said. "For this one here doesn't understand something about what I've been saying, but he says that he supposes Menexenus knows, and he bids me to ask him."

"Then why don't you ask?" he said.

"But I will ask," I said. "Tell me, Menexenus, whatever I ask you. Now it happens that since I was a boy I've desired a certain possession, just as others desire other things. For one desires to acquire horses, another dogs, another gold, and another honors. Now me, I'm of a gentle disposition regarding

e

these things, but when it comes to the acquisition of friends I'm quite passionately in love; and I would like to have[32] a good friend rather than the best quail or cock to be found among humans, and indeed, by Zeus, for my part, rather than a horse or a dog. And I suppose, by the Dog, that I would much rather acquire a companion than the gold of Darius,[33] and rather than Darius himself—that's the kind of lover of 12a companions I am.[34] So when I see you, you and Lysis, I am struck by it and I congratulate you on your happiness in that, young as you are, you [two] are able to acquire this possession quickly and easily, and that you have quickly and thoroughly acquired such a friend in him, and he, again, in you. But I am so far from the possession that I don't even know the manner in which one becomes a friend of another, but these are the very things I wish to ask of you, since you are experienced. Now tell me: When someone loves someone, which one be-
b comes a friend of the other, the one who loves[35] of the loved, or the loved one of the lover? Or is there no difference?"

"There seems to be no difference, in my opinion," he said.

"How do you mean?" I said. "Do both become friends of each other if only the one loves the other?"

"That's my opinion," he said.

"What? Isn't it possible for someone to love but not to be loved in return by the one whom he loves?"

"It is."

"And what about this? Isn't it possible for one who loves even to be hated? For example, the opinion is held, I suppose, that even passionate lovers sometimes suffer this from their
c favorites. For though they love as much as possible, some of them suppose that they're not loved in return, and some that they're even hated. Or isn't this true, in your opinion?"

"Very true indeed," he said.

"Then in such a case," I said, "the one loves, and the other is loved?"

"Yes."

"Then which of them is a friend of the other? Is it the one who loves [that is a friend] of the loved—whether he is in fact loved in return or whether he is even hated—or is it the loved one, of the lover? Or again, in such a situation is neither one a friend of the other unless they both love each other?"

d   "That's how it seems, at any rate."

"Now, then, our opinion is different from what it was before. For then, if the one were to love, they were both friends,[36] in our opinion; whereas now it is that neither is a friend unless they both love."

"I'm afraid so," he said.

"And so nothing which does not love in return is a friend[37] to the lover."

"It doesn't seem so."

"Therefore, those whom horses don't love in return are not lovers of horses, and those [whom quail don't love in return] are not lovers of quail; nor, again, are they lovers of dogs, lovers of wine, lovers of gymnastics, or lovers of wisdom,[38] unless wisdom loves them in return. Or do each of them love

e   these things, although the things are not friends,[39] and was the poet speaking falsely when he said,

> Prosperous is he who has children as friends,[40]
>   together with single-hoofed horses,
> Dogs for the hunt, and a guest-friend[41] in a foreign
>   land"?[42]

"No he wasn't, not in my opinion at least," he said.

"But in your opinion he was speaking the truth?"

"Yes."

"That which is loved, therefore, is a friend to the lover, as it seems, Menexenus, whether it loves or even if it hates. Newly-born children, for example—some of whom don't yet love, while others even hate, whenever they're chastised by their mother or by their father—despite even their hating, are nevertheless at that time, most of all, dearest to their parents."

"That's how it is, in my opinion," he said.

"By this account, therefore, it's not the one who loves who is a friend, but the loved one."

"It seems so."

"And so the hated one is an enemy, but not the one who hates."[43]

"So it appears."

"Many, therefore, are loved by their enemies and hated by their friends, and they are friends to their enemies and enemies to their friends, if that which is loved is a friend, and not that which loves. And yet it is very unreasonable, my dear companion—or rather, I suppose, it is even impossible—to be an enemy to one's friend or a friend to one's enemy."

"What you say seems true, Socrates," he said.

"Then if this is impossible, that which loves would be a friend of the loved."

"So it appears."

"And so, in turn, that which hates would be an enemy of the hated."

"Necessarily."

"Therefore, it will follow that we must necessarily agree to the same things as we did before, namely that often there is a friend of a non-friend, and often, in fact, of an enemy, whenever someone either loves something that does not love or else loves something that hates. And often there is an enemy of a non-enemy, or indeed, of a friend, whenever someone either hates something that does not hate or else hates something that loves."[44]

"I'm afraid so," he said.

"What, then, shall we make of it," I said, "if neither those who love, nor the loved ones, nor those who both love and are loved will be friends? Or shall we say that there are still some others, aside from these, who become friends to each other?"

"By Zeus, Socrates," he said, "for my part I can't find my way at all."

d "Can it be, Menexenus," I said, "that we were seeking in an altogether incorrect fashion?"

"Yes—at least in my opinion, Socrates," said Lysis. And at the same time as he said this he blushed. I had the opinion that what had been spoken escaped him involuntarily, because of his applying his mind intensely to what was being said—an attitude which was evident also while he was listening. And so, since I wished to give Menexenus a rest and was also pleased

e by that one's love of wisdom,[45] I turned to Lysis and began to make my arguments to him.[46] And I said, "Lysis, in my opinion what you say is true, that if we had been examining correctly, we would never have wandered so. But let's not go in that direction any longer, for indeed that examination appears to me like a quite difficult path. Instead, we need to go on, in my opinion, from where we turned aside—by examining the

214a things according to the poets.[47] For the poets are, as it were, our fathers in wisdom and our guides. And surely it is in no inferior fashion that they speak about friends and declare their view of who they happen to be. On the contrary, they assert that the god himself makes them friends, by leading them to each other. And they say these things, I suppose, in a manner somewhat like this,

> Always a god leads [the one who is] like to [the one who is] like[48]

b and makes him acquainted. Or don't you happen to have come across these verses?"

"I have," he said.

"Then do you also happen to have come across the writings of the wisest ones, which say these very things, namely that what is like is always necessarily a friend to its like? And they, I suppose, are the ones who converse and write about nature and the whole."

"What you say is true," he said.

"And so," I said, "do they speak well?"

"Perhaps," he said.

"Perhaps in half of it," I said. "Or perhaps even in all, only we don't understand them. For in our opinion the nearer the
c one who is wicked comes to the wicked and the more he associates with him, the more hated he becomes. For he does injustice. And in our opinion, presumably, it's impossible for those who do and suffer injustice to be friends. Isn't that so?"

"Yes," he said.

"In this way, then, half of what is said would not be true, if indeed those who are wicked are like each other."

"What you say is true."

"But in my opinion, they mean that those who are good are alike and are friends to each other, while those who are bad—as is in fact said about them—are never alike, not even them-
d selves to themselves, but are impulsive and unsteady. And

what is itself unlike and at variance with itself would hardly become like or a friend to anything else. Or isn't this also your opinion?"

"It is mine," he said.

"This then, my companion, is in my opinion what they are hinting at when they say that what is like is a friend to its like, namely that he who is good is a friend to the good—he alone to him[49] alone—while he who is bad never enters into true friendship either with good or with bad. Do you share this opinion?"

He nodded assent.

"So now, then, we've gotten hold of who are friends. For
e   the argument indicates to us that it is [all] those who are good."

"Very much so, in my opinion," he said.

"And in mine," I said. "And yet I'm uneasy about something in it. Come now, in the name of Zeus,[50] let us see what it is that I suspect. Is he who is like, insofar as he is like, a friend to his like, and is such a one useful to such a one? Or consider, rather, in the following way. Would anything whatsoever which is like anything whatsoever have the power to hold out any benefit to it, or to do it any harm, which that couldn't also do itself to itself? Or would it have the power to suffer anything [from its like] which it couldn't also suffer
215a from itself? How then, would such things be treasured by each other, if they held out to each other no help as allies? Is that possible?"

"No it isn't."

"And how would what was not treasured be a friend?"

"There is no way."

"But then he who is like is not a friend to his like. Yet might he who is good be a friend to the good insofar as he is good—not insofar as he is like?"

"Perhaps."

"What? Wouldn't he who is good, insofar as he is good, be to that extent sufficient for himself?"

"Yes."

"And he who is sufficient would be in want of nothing, in accordance with his sufficiency."

"Well, how could he not be?"

b "And whoever is in want of nothing would not treasure anything, either."

"Certainly not."

"And whoever would not treasure would also not love."

"Surely not."

"And whoever doesn't love is not a friend."

"It doesn't appear so."

"How, then, in our view will those who are good be at all friends to the good,[51] since neither do they long for each other when absent—for even apart they are sufficient for themselves—nor do they have any use for each other[52] when present? What device is there for those who are of such a kind to make much of each other?"

"None," he said.

c "And if they don't make much of each other, they wouldn't be friends."

"That's true."

"Consider, then, Lysis, where we have gone astray. Are we somehow being deceived in the whole?"[53]

"How could that be?" he said.

"I once heard someone—and I just now recollect it—saying that what is like was most hostile to its like, and that those who are good [were most hostile] to the good. And moreover, he brought Hesiod forward as a witness, saying that,

Potter bears a grudge against potter, and singer against
singer,

d   And beggar against beggar[54]

and indeed in everything else he said it was likewise necessary
for things most alike to be most filled with envy, love of victory, and hatred toward each other, but for things most unlike [to be most filled] with friendship. For he who is poor, he
said, is compelled to be a friend to the wealthy, as is he who is
weak, to the strong—for the sake of help as an ally; and so it is
between the one who is ill and the doctor, and in all things
whoever doesn't know is compelled to treasure the knower

e   and to love him. And indeed, he kept pursuing his argument[55]
still further and more magnificently, saying that what is like
was wholly removed from being a friend to its like, but that
the situation was rather the very opposite of this. For that
which is most opposite, he said, is most a friend to the most
opposite; that is to say, each thing desires what is of such a
kind, and not its like; namely, what is dry desires [something]
wet, what is cold [something] hot, what is bitter [something]
sweet, and what is sharp [something] blunt, while what is
empty desires filling and what is full emptying, and the other
things likewise according to the same account; for what is opposite, he said, is sustenance to its opposite; for what is like

216a would enjoy no advantage from its like. And indeed, my companion, it was my opinion, while he was saying these things,
that he was clever. For he spoke well. But as for you
[plural]," I said, "what's your opinion of how he spoke?"

"That he spoke well," said Menexenus, "at least so it seems
from hearing it like this."

"Shall we then assert that what is opposite is most a friend
to its opposite?"

"Very much so."

"Well," I said, "isn't that strange, Menexenus? And won't these all-wise men, the ones skilled in contradicting, be
b pleased to leap upon us straightway and ask whether hatred isn't most opposite to friendship? What shall we answer them? Or isn't it necessary to agree that they're speaking the truth?"

"It's necessary."

" 'Well, then,' they will say, 'is that which is an enemy a friend to the friend, or is that which is a friend [a friend] to the enemy?' "

"Neither," he said.

"But is that which is just a friend to the unjust; or what is moderate, to the undisciplined; or what is good, to the bad?"

"That wouldn't be the case, in my opinion."

"But yet," I said, "if something is indeed a friend to its friend by way of opposition, even these things are necessarily friends."

"Necessarily."

"Therefore, neither is what is like a friend to its like, nor is what is opposite a friend to its opposite."

"It doesn't seem so."

c "And let us also examine this further point. Perhaps what is truly a friend escapes our notice even more, and it may be none of these things; but rather whatever is neither good nor bad may thus at some times become a friend of the good."

"How do you mean?" he said.

"Well, by Zeus," I said, "I don't know, but I am really dizzy myself from the perplexity of the argument, and I'm afraid—as the old saying goes—that what is beautiful is a friend.[56] It seems, at any rate, like something soft, smooth,
d and sleek. And that is why, perhaps, it easily slides past us and

gives us the slip, inasmuch as it is such. For I say that the good
is beautiful. And you, don't you suppose so?"

"I do indeed."

"And so, I say through divination that whatever is neither
good nor bad is a friend of the beautiful and good.[57] Listen to
what I have in view in speaking as a diviner. In my opinion
there are, as it were, some three kinds—that which is good,
that which is bad, and that which is neither good nor bad.
And what's your opinion?"

"That's mine too," he said.

e

"And in my opinion neither is what is good a friend to the
good, nor is what is bad [a friend] to the bad, nor is what is
good, to the bad—just as the previous argument doesn't allow
it. There is left, then, if indeed anything is a friend to
anything, that whatever is neither good nor bad is a friend
either of the good or of what is such as it is itself. For
nothing, surely, would become a friend to the bad."

"That's true."

"But we also said just now that what is like is not a friend
to its like. Didn't we?"

"Yes."

"Therefore, to whatever is neither good nor bad, that
which is such as it is itself will not be a friend."

"It doesn't appear so."

217a

"It follows, therefore, that whatever is neither good nor
bad becomes a friend to the good—that alone to it alone."

"Necessarily, as it seems."

"Well, boys," I said, "and is what is now being said guiding us in a fine way? If we were willing to conceive of the
healthy body, at any rate, it has no want of the medical art or
of benefit. For its condition is sufficient, so that no one when

he is healthy is a friend to a doctor because of his health. Isn't that so?"

"No one."

"Rather, I suppose, the one who is ill, because of his disease [would be his friend]."

"Well, how could he not be?"

b "Now disease is a bad thing, and the medical art is a beneficial and good one."

"Yes."

"And a body, presumably—insofar as it is a body—is neither good nor bad."

"That's so."

"And a body is compelled because of disease to welcome and to love the medical art."

"Yes, in my opinion."

"Then whatever is neither bad nor good becomes a friend of the good because of the presence of an evil."[58]

"It seems so."

"And it is clear that this is before it itself becomes bad as a result of the evil which it has. For once it had become bad, it c would no longer have any desire for, or be a friend of, the good.[59] For we said that it was impossible for bad to be a friend to good."

"Yes, impossible."

"Now examine for yourselves what I say. For I say that some things are also themselves of such a kind as whatever is present, whereas some are not. For example, if someone were willing to rub anything whatsoever with any coloring, I suppose that [the coloring] which is rubbed on is present to that which it's rubbed upon."

"Very much so."

"Then is that which is rubbed upon of such a kind, at that time, with respect to color, as what is on it?"

d   "I don't understand," he said.

"Well, consider as follows," I said. "If someone should rub your hair—which is blond—with white lead, would it at that time be white, or would it appear so?"

"It would appear so," he said.

"And yet whiteness would be present to it."

"Yes."

"But nevertheless, your hair would not yet be any the more white; but though whiteness is present, it is not at all either white or black."

"That's true."

"But when, my friend, old age brings this same color to it, it becomes at that time of such a kind as what is present—white by the presence of white."

e   "Well, how could it not?"

"This, then, is what I'm now asking, if whenever anything is present to something, that which has it will be of such a kind as what is present. Or will it be so if the something is present in a certain way, and if not, not?"

"It's rather the latter," he said.

"And therefore, whatever is neither bad nor good is sometimes not yet bad although an evil is present, but there are times when it has already become such."[60]

"Very much so."

"Then whenever it is not yet bad, though an evil is present, this presence makes it desire good. But the presence which makes it bad deprives it of the desire, at the same time as the 218a   friendship, of the good. For no longer is it neither bad nor good, but it is bad. And a good thing, as we showed, is not a friend to a bad one."[61]

"Certainly not."

"Because of these things, then, we might say also that the ones who are already wise, whether these are gods or human beings, no longer love wisdom.[62] Nor, on the other hand, would we say that those love wisdom who have ignorance in such a manner as to be bad. For we wouldn't say that anyone bad and stupid loves wisdom. There are left, then, those who while having this evil, ignorance, are not yet senseless or

b   stupid as a result of it, but still regard themselves as not knowing whatever they don't know. And so therefore, the ones who are not yet either good nor bad love wisdom; but as many as are bad do not love wisdom, and neither do those who are good. For it appeared to us in our previous arguments that neither is what is opposite a friend of its opposite, nor is what is like a friend of its like. Or don't you [plural] remember?"

"Very much so," they [both] said.

"We have now, then," I said, "Lysis and Menexenus, most certainly discovered that which is the friend and [that which] isn't. For we assert—regarding the soul, and regarding the

c   body, and everywhere—that whatever is neither bad nor good is itself, because of the presence of an evil, a friend of the good."

They [both] entirely assented and granted that this was so. And what is more, I rejoiced greatly myself, as if I were a hunter and had, to my satisfaction, what I had been hunting [for myself]. But then some most strange suspicion came over me—from where, I don't know—that the things we had agreed to were not true, and at once I said in vexation, "Woe is me, Lysis and Menexenus! I'm afraid it was a dream that we've been wealthy."

d   "Why do you say that?" said Menexenus.

"I'm afraid," I said, "that we have come across some false arguments about the friend—[false] like boastful human beings."

"Well, how is that?" he said.

"Let us look," I said, "in this way. Is he who would be a friend a friend to someone,[63] or is he not?"

"Necessarily," he said.

"Now is it for the sake of nothing, and because of nothing, or else for the sake of something,[64] and because of something?"

"For the sake of something and because of something."

"Now that thing, for the sake of which the one who is a friend is a friend to his friend, is it a friend,[65] or is it neither a friend nor an enemy?"

e   "I don't quite follow," he said.

"That's to be expected," I said. "But perhaps you will follow in this manner, and I suppose that even I will know better what I mean. The one who is ill, as we were saying just now, is a friend of the doctor. Isn't that so?"

"Yes."

"Is he, then, a friend of the doctor because of disease and for the sake of health?"

"Yes."

"And is disease an evil?"

"How could it not be?"

"And what about health?" I said. "Is it a good or an evil or neither?"

"A good," he said.

219a   "We were saying, then, as it seems, that the body, which is neither good nor bad, is because of disease—that is, because of what is bad—a friend of the medical art; and the medical art is a good. And the medical art has accepted the friendship for the sake of health, and health is a good. Isn't that so?"

"Yes."

"And is health a friend or not a friend?"

"A friend."

"And is disease an enemy?"[66]

"Very much so."

b   "That which is neither bad nor good, therefore, is a friend of the good because of what is bad and what is an enemy, and for the sake of the good and friend."

"It appears so."

"That which is a friend, therefore, is a friend for the sake of the friend,[67] and because of that which is its enemy."

"It seems so."

"Well," I said. "Since we have arrived here, boys, let us apply our minds lest we be deceived. For that that which is a friend has become a friend of the friend, and [that] that which is like becomes a friend of its like—which we assert to be impossible—this I allow to go by. But nevertheless, let us examine this following matter, so that what is now being said

c   doesn't deceive us. The medical art, we assert, is a friend for the sake of health."

"Yes."

"Health, then, is also a friend?"

"Very much so."

"If, therefore, it is a friend, it is for the sake of something."

"Yes."

"Now, that something is a friend, if it is going to follow our previous agreement."

"Very much so."

"Will that too, then, also be a friend for the sake of a friend?"

"Yes."

"Isn't it necessary, then, for us to renounce going on like this or else[68] to arrive at some beginning principle, which will no longer bring us back to another friend, but will have come to that which is a friend in the first place,[69] and for the sake of which we say that the other things are also all friends?"

"It's necessary."

"This, then, is what I mean. I suspect that all the other things which we say are friends for the sake of that—being some phantoms, as it were, of that—are deceiving us, and I suspect that it is that first thing which is truly a friend. Now let us conceive of it in this manner. Whenever someone makes much of something—as sometimes a father values his son more highly than all his other possessions—would such a one also make much of something else for the sake of [70] considering his son worth everything? For example, if he should become aware that his son had drunk hemlock, would he make much of wine, if he considered that this would save his son?"

"Of course," he said.

"And also of the vessel in which the wine was contained?"

"Very much so."

"At that time, then, would he make no more of either one—neither an earthenware cup nor his own son—and no more of either three *kotylai*[71] of wine nor of his own son? Or is it somewhat like this? All such seriousness is not directed to those things which are provided for the sake of something, but to that for the sake of which all such things are provided. Not that we don't often claim to make much of gold and silver. But I suspect that it's none the more so in truth. Rather, that is what we regard as everything—whatever it comes to light as being—namely that for the sake of which gold and all provisions are provided. Shall we not speak in this way?"

"Very much so."

"Then is it also the same account about the friend? For it is manifest that we say 'friend' in name only as regards all those things which we assert to be friends to us for the sake of some other friend.[72] For I'm afraid that what is really a friend is that itself into which all these so-called friendships terminate."

"I'm afraid that's so," he said.

"Then what is really a friend is not a friend for the sake of some friend?"

"That's true."

"This, then, has been dismissed—the view that what is a friend is a friend for the sake of some friend. But then is that which is good a friend?"

"That's my opinion."

"Then is what is good loved because of what is bad, and is the situation as follows? If, of the three beings which we were just now speaking of—good, and bad, and neither good nor bad—the two of them were left and what is bad should get out of the way and lay hold of neither any body, nor any soul, nor any of the other things which we assert to be, themselves in themselves, neither bad nor good, would what is good be in no way useful to us at that time, and would it have become useless? For if nothing were to harm us any longer, we would require no benefit at all, and thus it would become manifest then that we had been treasuring and loving what is good because of what is bad, as if that which is good were a drug for the bad, and what is bad were a disease. And if there is no disease, then a drug is not required. And as for what is good, is its nature like this and is it loved by us—who are in the middle of the bad and the good—because of what is bad, while it is of no use itself for its own sake?"

"That seems to be so," he said.

"Therefore, that friend to us, into which all the others
e   [were seen to] terminate—for we asserted that those things
were friends for the sake of another friend—has no
resemblance to them. For they have been called friends for the
sake of a friend, but what is really a friend comes to light as
being of a nature entirely the opposite of this. For it has appeared plainly to be a friend to us for the sake of an enemy,[73]
and if that which is an enemy would go away, it is no
longer,[74] as it seems, a friend to us."

"Not in my opinion," he said, "at least not to judge from
the way it's now being spoken of."

"In the name of Zeus,"[75] I said, "if that which is bad ceases
221a   to be, will there no longer be hungering or thirsting, or any
other such things? Or will there be hunger, if indeed there are
humans and the other living beings, but without its being
harmful? And will there be thirst, and the other desires, but
without their being bad, inasmuch as what is bad will have
ceased to be? Or is the question ludicrous—what will be or
will not be then? For who knows? But this, at any rate, we
do know, that even now it is possible for one who is hungry
to be harmed, and it is possible for him also to be benefited.
Isn't that so?"

"Very much so."

b   "Then is it also possible for one who is thirsty, and who has
all the other such desires, sometimes to desire beneficially, and
sometimes harmfully, and sometimes neither?"

"Exceedingly so."

"Then if the things which are bad are ceasing to be,[76] what
connection do they have with those which don't happen to be
bad, so that those should be ceasing to be together with the
evils?"

"None."

"There will be, then, whatever desires are neither good nor bad, even if the things which are bad cease to be."

"It appears so."

"Now is it possible for one who desires and who loves passionately[77] not to love[78] [as a friend] that which he desires and loves passionately?"

"Not in my opinion, at any rate."

c "There will be, then, as it seems, some [things that are] friends, even if evils cease to be."

"Yes."

"Yet if what is bad were a cause of a thing's being a friend, and it ceased to be, nothing would be a friend to another. For if a cause ceased to be, I suppose it would be impossible for there still to be that [thing] which had this cause."

"You are speaking correctly."

"Now have we agreed that what is a friend loves something and because of something? And did we suppose at that time that whatever is neither good nor bad loves what is good because of what is bad?"

"That's true."

d "But now, as it seems, there appears some other cause of loving and being loved."

"It seems so."

"Then is desire, as we were just now saying, really a cause of friendship? And is what desires a friend to that which it desires and at the time when it desires? And as for that which we were previously saying to be a friend, was it some kind of idle talk, like a long poem strung together?"

"I'm afraid so," he said.

"Now surely," I said, "that which desires desires whatever e it is in want of. Isn't that so?"

"Yes."

"Is what is in want, therefore, a friend of that which it is in want of?"

"That's my opinion."

"And it comes to be in want of whatever it is somehow deprived of."[79]

"How could it not?"

"It appears, then, Menexenus and Lysis, that passionate love, friendship, and desire happen to be for what is akin,[80] as it seems."

They [both] assented.

"You, therefore, if you are[81] friends to each other, are by nature in some way akin to each other."[82]

"Just so," they [both] said.

222a   "And therefore," I said, "if someone desires another, boys, or loves him passionately, he would never desire, nor love passionately, nor love [as a friend] unless he happened to be akin in some way to his passionately beloved—either in his soul, or else in some character of his soul, or some of its ways, or some aspect[83] of it."

"Very much so," said Menexenus. But Lysis was silent.

"Well," I said, "it has come to light as necessary for us to love what is akin by nature."

"It seems so," he said.

"It is necessary, therefore, for the passionate lover who is genuine, and not pretended, to be loved by his favorite(s)."[84]

b   Now [both] Lysis and Menexenus, with difficulty, somehow nodded yes, but Hippothales radiated all sorts of colors as a result of his pleasure. And wishing to examine the argument [for myself], I said, "Lysis and Menexenus, if what is akin differs in some respect from the like, we might be saying something, in my opinion, concerning what a friend is. But if it happens that like and akin are the same, it isn't easy to reject the previous argument, which says that what is like is useless to its like insofar as there is likeness. And it is out of tune to

c agree that what is useless is a friend. Do you wish, then," I said, "since we are drunk, as it were, from the argument, for us to grant and to declare that what is akin is something other than the like?"

"Very much so."

"Shall we also, then, posit that what is good is akin to everyone,[85] and that what is bad is alien? Or else [shall we posit] that what is bad is akin to the bad; that what is good is akin to the good; and that whatever is neither good nor bad is akin to whatever is neither good nor bad?"

d They [both] said that in their opinion each was thus akin to each.

"And so, boys," I said, "we have fallen back into those accounts concerning friendship which we rejected at first. For he who is unjust will be no less a friend to the unjust—as will he who is bad, to the bad—than he who is good, to the good."

"It seems so," he said.

"And what about this? If we declare what is good and what is akin to be the same, then isn't only he who is good a friend, [a friend] to the good?"

"Very much so."

"But yet on this point, too, we supposed that we had refuted ourselves. Or don't you [plural] remember?"

"We remember."

e "What, then, might we still make of the argument? Or is there clearly nothing? Well, in any case I want to count up all the things which have been mentioned, as those who are wise in the law courts do. For if neither the loved ones, nor those who love, nor those who are like, nor those who are unlike, nor those who are good, nor those who are akin, nor as many other things as we have gone through—for I, at least, don't remember any more because of their multitude—if nothing among these is a friend, I no longer know what to say."

223a   But as I said these things, I already had in mind to set in motion someone else among the older fellows. But then, like some daemons, the attendants—the one of Menexenus and the one of Lysis—came forward, bringing their brothers. And they called to them, and bade them to leave for home. For it was already late. Now at first, we and those standing around tried to drive them away. Yet since they paid no heed to us, but showed irritation and kept calling out none the

b   less with a somewhat foreign accent—and in our opinion they had been drinking quite a bit at the Hermaea, so there seemed to be no way to approach them—we were therefore defeated by them, and we broke up our group. But nevertheless, as they were already going away, I said, "Now, Lysis and Menexenus, we have become ridiculous—I, an old man, and you. For these fellows will say, as they go away, that we suppose we're one another's friends—for I also put myself among you—but what he who is a friend is we have not yet been able to discover."[86]

Notes to the Translation

1. Both the Academy and the Lyceum were among the exercise fields located just outside of Athens. These "gymnasia" also served as the locations for schools even before Plato and Aristotle made them famous by teaching there.

2. Panops is the name of an Athenian "hero," or local deity. His name, taken literally, may mean "all-seeing."

3. Paeania is one of the demes, or townships, of ancient Athens.

4. Or, "But it's fitting [that you do so]."

5. The word *kalos,* which is here translated as "good-looking," will also be translated as "fine" (cf. 204a4) and "beautiful." In addition to the various usual senses of the English word "beautiful," it often means something like "admirable" or even "noble."

6. A palaestra was a kind of wrestling school, though other kinds of instruction took place there as well.

7. The word here translated as "speeches" is in Greek *logoi* (*logos* in the singular). *Logos* can also mean "discourse," "argument," or "conversation," as well as "reason." It is both speech and the thought which is articulated and understood through speech. In this translation it is rendered as "speech," "argument," or "account," except on one occasion (206c5), where the plural *logoi* will be rendered as "discussion."

8. The name Miccus means, literally, "small."

9. The word *hikanos,* which is here translated as "capable," will be rendered elsewhere (except at 209d5) as "sufficient." "Capable," or "competent," is an obsolete meaning of the English word "sufficient."

10. The words that are translated in this paragraph (as at 204e10, 205a1, and 206a1–2) by "love," "lover," and "beloved" are all related to the Greek *erōs,* which refers primarily to passionate sexual love. Though it is

53

most natural to translate this family of words simply as "love," or "to love," etc., they will be translated later in the dialogue (from 211e) as "passionate love," or "to love passionately," etc. This change is necessary in order to distinguish these words from those related to the Greek *philein*, a key word in this dialogue, which also means "to love." For further discussion see note 22.

11. He is called, that is, "Son of Democrates." See, for example, 207b8 and 209a5.

12. *To eidos*, which means primarily the "look" or "looks" of a thing, is the same word commonly translated by "idea" or "form" in Plato's so-called "Theory of Ideas." For the kinship between the ordinary and the philosophic uses of this word, see Jacob Klein, *A Commentary on Plato's "Meno"* (Chapel Hill, 1965), pp. 49–51.

13. Aexone, like Paeania, was a deme of Athens.

14. The word *gennaion*, which is translated as "noble" here, at 207c3, and at 209a1–2, also conveys the sense "from a distinguished family."

15. Or, "made." The same word, *poieō*, is translated here as "to make [poems]" and also "to compose."

16. "Deme": See note 3.

17. The Hermaea was a festival in honor of the god Hermes, who was—among his other attributes—patron of the palaestra.

18. *Astragaloi*, or knucklebones, are small bones from the joints of an animal's feet. They were used like dice.

19. *Kalos te kagathos*, which is literally translated as "beautiful and good," was commonly thought of as a single notion, somewhat akin to the English word "gentleman." This phrase was used in the neuter plural at 205e6. See also 216d3–4.

20. The word is *gennaioteros*, which may also mean "of a more distinguished family." See note 14.

21. Here for the first time Socrates uses the dual number, which is distinct from the plural and which can be used with nouns, adjectives, pronouns, and the second and third persons of verbs. The use of the dual, which is a rare form in Attic Greek, implies that two persons or things are being thought of together as a pair. Because of its importance in this dialogue about friendship, subsequent uses of the dual number will be marked by the addition in brackets of the word "both" or the word "two," although these bracketed words do not appear in the Greek. Here, how-

ever, and also at 212d2, the word for "both" appears explicitly (in the dual form) in Greek.

22. Here is the first occurrence of the verb *philein*, corresponding to the noun *philos*, or "friend." Its meaning is something like "to be related to another as a friend." No English word except "to love" adequately translates *philein*, although on some occasions "to love" will have to be understood in an attenuated sense, as in the phrase "to love wine." The difficulty with this translation is that previously the words "love," "lover," and "beloved" were used as translations of the Greek *erōs* (*erastēs, erōmenos*, etc.), which refers primarily—and in this dialogue—to passionate sexual love. To lessen confusion, the words "to love" "loved one," "lover of," etc., will be reserved—from this point on in the dialogue—as translations of the Greek *philein* (*philoumenos*, etc.). After this, whenever *erōs* and related words appear in the text, they will be translated "passionate love," "to love passionately," etc. The word "love" by itself will no longer be used as a translation for *erōs*. *Erōs* is the theme of Plato's *Symposium*, where it is spoken of as a god (or a demigod).

23. The verb *diakōluein*, which is here and subsequently translated as "to prevent," may also mean "to hinder."

24. *Paidagōgos* means literally "one who leads a boy." The Athenian *paidagōgos* was typically a slave who attended boys to and from school and who watched over them while there.

25. See note 9.

26. The word *philos*, which is here translated as "dear," is an adjective related to the word for "friend." In prose, at least, it is almost always passive rather than active in sense, and it means "dear to" rather than "fond of." But this adjective is identical in spelling to the noun which means "friend." Indeed, it can be difficult at times to know whether the word is being used as an adjective or as a noun. Moreover, since the *Lysis* as a whole is devoted to the question of what it is to be (a) *philos*, I have tried to approach uniformity in translating this key word. The need for this uniformity is especially evident in the passage from 212a9 to 213c8, where the question is asked whether the *philos* is the one who loves, the loved one (that is, the dear one), or the one who both loves and is loved. Accordingly, I use the translation "friend," rather than "dear," in all subsequent cases. I do this even though in some passages the sense "dear" is almost certainly the intended one—for example, where the word is used of things in-

stead of persons. Therefore, even health and the art of medicine will be spoken of as "friends" (219a5, c1; consider, however, 219a4). Yet as these examples indicate, the context will enable the reader to see for himself when the word "friend" is being extended beyond its normal English sense. Of further help is the fact that the two phrases "friend of" and "friend to," whenever they appear in the translation, correspond to distinct Greek phrases. In the former case, the word *philos* is almost certainly a noun and active (if not also passive) in sense. In the latter case, however, it is presumably an adjective with the passive sense of "dear."

27. I have here translated the word *nous* by "good sense," although elsewhere it appears only in the phrases "to apply one's mind," or "to have in mind."

28. *Oikeion,* or "akin," is closely related to the word *oikia*—"house," "household," or "home." *Hoi oikeioi* are primarily "those who dwell with one," and the word usually refers to one's relatives. The meaning of the neuter *oikeion* ranges from something like "one's own" to something like "appropriate or suitable to a thing." Because of its importance in this dialogue, the word *oikeion* will always be translated as "akin," although the alternative rendering "one's own" should also be kept in mind.

29. The same Greek verb, *phronein,* which was translated in Socrates' previous question by "to be thinking" is here rendered by "to be thoughtful." The related adjective, *phronimos,* was translated as "prudent" at 210b1.

30. Or, "playfully."

31. *Deinos,* or "terrifying," is elsewhere translated by the more colloquial "dreadful." It originally suggests something of the strange and the uncanny. On other occasions, and perhaps here as well, it means merely "clever." One who is *deinos legein* is a clever, that is a dangerous, speaker.

32. Or, more literally, "I would wish that there come into being for me. . . ."

33. Darius II was the Great King of Persia from 424 to 406 B.C. The Persian king was thought to be the wealthiest man in the world (see *Alcibiades I,* 123a6).

34. See note 22. Also, the word here translated as "lover of companions" is not used by Socrates in its most usual sense, which is rather "fond of one's [present] companions" or even "loyal to one's companions."

35. I have attempted to preserve in English, even at the price of some

awkwardness, the distinctions between important Greek words—in particular, words preceded by a definite article—which differ only in gender. Moreover, where there is an ambiguity of the Greek gender, I have tried not to impose a decision of my own. While many such ambiguities may be mere accidents of Greek grammar, I leave it to the reader's judgment to distinguish between those which are intended and those where the context leaves no room for serious doubt which gender is meant. The translations of key words with a masculine definite article will be of the form "he who loves (is good, is a friend, etc.)," "the one who loves (is good, is a friend, etc.)," and "the loved one," etc. Where the definite article is neuter, the standard expressions will be "that which loves (is good, is a friend, etc.)," "what is good (a friend, etc.)," "that which is loved," or "what is loved." Where the Greek article is ambiguous—typically in the genitive or dative case—the standard translations will be "the lover," "the good," "the friend," and "the loved." The reader should be reminded, however, that the neuter form *philon,* where it lacks a definite article, is translated as "a friend," rather than "a dear thing," for the reasons given in note 26. Since gods as well as human beings are spoken of in the masculine gender, I cannot substitute "a man who loves," for example, in the place of "he who loves."

36. The word for "both" and the word for "friends" appear in the Greek in the dual number; cf. note 21.

37. This is the first occurrence of the neuter form of the word for "friend." In this and similar passages, the alternative rendering "dear" should be especially born in mind. See notes 26 and 35.

38. Or, "philosophers."

39. Or, "although the things are not dear. . . ." See note 26.

40. This translation reflects Socrates' apparent interpretation of the passage. A closer approximation to Solon's intended meaning would be, "Prosperous is he who has *dear* children, single-hoofed horses, etc." In this latter interpretation, the phrase "dear children" may mean little more than "children of his own."

41. *Xenos,* or "guest-friend," is a word referring to foreigners who give and receive kindly treatment to each other—both "hosts" and "guests." In particular, it refers to those inhabitants of other cities with whom a man or a family would maintain a relation of reciprocal hospitality. This relationship was an important social tie.

42. These verses come from an elegy by Solon (Diehl, 13), and their original context is unknown. Solon, an Athenian who flourished almost two centuries before the imagined date of the conversation in the *Lysis,* was regarded as one of the Seven Wise Men of ancient Greece. He was also thought of, more than any other man, as *the* Athenian lawgiver. According to Aristotle (*The Athenian Constitution* 41.2), Athenian democracy had its beginning from the code of laws which Solon drew up.

43. In place of "the one who hates," which is read by modern editors, the manuscripts all contain the apparently unintelligible "the one who loves."

44. This is a translation of the reading selected by Burnet, as well as by most modern editors. The most reliable manuscripts, however, would have to be translated as follows: "whenever someone either loves something that hates or hates something that loves."

45. Or, "philosophy."

46. Or, "began to make my arguments with a view to him." The word translated as "arguments" is *logoi.* See note 7.

47. Some modern editors, following Heindorf, emend the text so as to read "by examining according to the poets." As for the manuscript version, which I have followed, it could perhaps also be translated, "by examining the things which are [i.e. exist] according to the poets."

48. *Odyssey* 17. 218. The text of the *Odyssey,* as it has come down to us, differs from Socrates' version by beginning with the word "as." It thus completes a thought begun in the previous line, which may be translated as follows: "Now most certainly is the bad guiding the bad." The speaker of these lines is Melantheus, a goatherd for Penelope's wicked suitors. Melantheus is addressing the swineherd Eumaeus and Odysseus himself, though the latter is disguised as a beggar.

49. Or, perhaps, "to it alone."

50. Or, perhaps, "you who are [descended] from Zeus." Cf. 205d1-2.

51. Or, as a secondary rendering, "How, then, will those who are good be at all friends to the good—that is, to us. . . ."

52. The word here translated by "each other" (*hautōn*) is not the most usual form of the reciprocal pronoun. More often, in fact, it is a reflexive pronoun, and it was used as such in this very sentence, where it was translated as "themselves." This ambiguous form is again used to mean "each other" at 215c1. The more usual form of the reciprocal pronoun ap-

pears, for example, at 215a1, 215a2, 215b5, and 215b7.

53. Or, "Are we being deceived by a certain whole?"

54. *Works and Days*, verses 25-26. These lines, as they appear in our text of Hesiod, differ somewhat from Socrates' version. A translation of the modern text would go as follows: "Potter bears a grudge against potter, and carpenter against carpenter,/And beggar is envious of beggar, and singer of singer."

55. The Greek word is *logos*. See note 7, and 215e8, 216c5.

56. See note 26. As for the saying itself, see Euripides, *Bacchae* 881, and Theognis, *Elegies* 17 ff.

57. See note 19.

58. *Kakon,* the word for "bad," also means "evil" or "an evil." The English words "bad" and "evil" will both be used as translations for the word *kakon,* and for that word alone.

59. This the reading of recent editors. The version in the manuscripts might be translated: "For once it had become bad, it would no longer, in any way, also be a friend of the good which it desired." Compare, however, 217e8-9.

60. It might be more literal to translate this last clause, "but there are times when what is of such a kind has already come into being."

61. Burnet, following a conjecture by Heindorf, has interchanged the positions of "good" and "bad" in this sentence. I do not follow his reading. Consider 217c1-2 and 216d8-e1.

62. Or, "philosophize." See note 38.

63. Or, possibly, "a friend to something."

64. These phrases could also be translated "for the sake of no one" and "for the sake of someone." Compare also 219c3. There can be no ambiguity, however, in the following sentence, which begins, "Now that *thing. . . .*"

65. See note 26. The alternative rendering "dear" should be kept in mind throughout this section of the dialogue.

66. Or, "something hated." The ambiguity between "enemy" and "hated" is analogous to that between "friend" and "dear." See note 26.

67. Burnet reads here ". . . is a friend *of the friend* for the sake of the friend." The addition of these three words has no manuscript authority, and I do not accept it.

68. The manuscripts read "and" here, instead of Burnet's "or else,"

which is a conjecture proposed originally by Schanz. Though I follow Burnet, the manuscript version is quite possibly correct.

69. A secondary rendering of this difficult phrase might be "but will be related to that which is a friend in the first place. . . ."

70. It would be perfectly acceptable, and even more plausible in the context, to translate this Greek word—*heneka*—as "on account of," or "as a result of." In this dialogue, however, Socrates has just made a clear and explicit distinction between *tou heneka*—"for the sake of something (good)"—and *dia ti*—"because of something (bad)." In other words, *to hou heneka* has meant the end which the "lover" has in view, while *to dia ho* has meant that (evil) whose presence is in part responsible for his pursuit of an absent good. Now in this passage, the phrase "considering his son to be worth everything" might indeed refer to an object of desire, rather than to the present situation for the worried father. The reader may judge for himself whether the distinction between these two prepositional phrases should be maintained here. The word *heneka* is also used at 220e4.

71. One *kotylos* equals approximately one-half pint.

72. Here I follow the reading of modern editors. According to the manuscripts, however, this sentence might be translated as follows: "For as regards all those things which we assert to be friends to us for the sake of some friend, it is manifest that we speak of it [i.e. the first friend] by means of a different word."

73. See note 70.

74. Or, "there is no longer. . . ."

75. Or, "from Zeus." See note 50.

76. Here, unlike at 220e7 and 221a4, Socrates uses the progressive aspect of the verb "to cease to be," and so the sentence might be translated as follows: "Then if the things which are bad are in the process of ceasing to be, what connection do they have with those which don't happen to be bad, so that those should be ceasing to be along with the evils?" In Socrates' next sentence (221b5–6), there are slight corruptions in the various manuscripts, but it is just possible that the verb "to cease to be" is progressive there as well. After that, however, Socrates' three following uses of the verb—the participles at 221c1, c3, and c4—are not progressive. The elimination of evils is there considered as having taken place once and for all.

77. *Erā.* See note 22.

78. *Philein.* See note 22.

79. The translation here follows Burnet's edition, which contains an emendation first proposed by Stephanus. The emended Greek might also be translated, "And it comes to be in want of whatever something is deprived of." The manuscripts, on the other hand, could be translated as follows: "And it comes to be in want of whatever (or whomever) someone is deprived of."

80. See note 28.

81. The verb "are" is here a dual form, though the same verb in the main clause of the sentence is plural. The personal pronoun "you" in this sentence, as well as the noun "friends," is a plural form rather than dual.

82. See note 52. The form of the reciprocal pronoun here is that one which can also be a reflexive pronoun.

83. The word here translated by "aspect" is *eidos.* See note 12. The three "parts" of the soul, as delineated in Book Four of Plato's *Republic,* are also called *eidē* of the soul. See, for example, *Republic* 440e8–441a3.

84. The Greek word for "favorite" is itself a plural form, and the choice between singular and plural must depend upon the context. Elsewhere, except for 212b8, the word has been translated by the more usual "favorite."

85. Or, "akin to everything."

86. Or, perhaps more literally, "we have not yet *become* able to discover." This final phrase might also be translated as follows: "but we have not yet been able to discover that he who is a friend is [i.e. exists]."

Plato's Dialogue
on Friendship

The Title and the Interlocutors

Lysis, the title of Plato's dialogue on friendship, is also a proper name designating one of the participants in the conversation. And even apart from the title, Lysis would be the first to attract our attention, for he is conspicuously beautiful, and descended from a noble and wealthy Athenian family. Moreover, his demeanor allows Socrates to see at a glance that he is outstanding not merely as a beauty but as a gentleman (*kalos te kagathos,* 207a3). Lysis seems to be a model of a boy, and especially is he a model son. He is so devoted to his family that his lover Hippothales tries to endear himself by singing praises of his ancestors. Lysis' attachment to his parents, in particular, is supported by the generous belief that even when they deny him things, they are acting from an intelligent and loving concern for his happiness. Since he holds this belief, he is a dutiful son, and his love for his parents goes together with an unquestioning obedience.

The above characterization of Lysis emerges early in the dialogue. At its end, however, he is seen engaging in a minor rebellion against his family's authority. For when the family slaves arrive to escort him and his friend Menexenus to their homes, Socrates and the boys try to drive them away. This little brawl between Socrates' circle and two somewhat drunken slaves is—with the possible exception of the end of the *Phaedo* (118a12)—the most violent scene in Plato's dialogues. Now it

goes without saying that this comic little rebellion proves un-
successful. But nonetheless, the effect of Socrates' conversation has been to undermine somehow Lysis' implicit accep-
tance of paternal rule. Socrates' conversation about friendship
seems to initiate a change in the character of the friendship
between Lysis and his parents. For this reason, among others,
it may be significant that the title *Lysis* is also a Greek word
meaning a "releasing," as in a releasing from chains.

Socrates' explicit inquiry into the question "what is a
friend?" is addressed to Lysis together with his friend Menexenus. It is appropriate that he discuss friendship with two
boys, for the young seem to be especially given to friendship
and especially fond of their friends. Moreover, Lysis and
Menexenus are not merely friends, but closest friends
(206d4–5). And we tend to consider friendship between two
—such as that between Achilles and Patroclus—to be the
truest kind.[1] Accordingly, Lysis and Menexenus would appear
to have the experience needed for a knowledgeable conversation about friends (cf. 212a7).

It is, however, Socrates, and not the boys, who initiates the
thematic inquiry. Friendship is a topic of conversation not
only because the boys may know about it, but also and more
immediately because it has become something questionable to
Socrates. According to Socrates' account, his own puzzling
experience is that despite a lifelong desire to acquire friends, he
has not yet acquired even one. This is a strange admission
from Socrates, for he seems to have been uncannily gifted in
acquiring friends. Indeed, the conclusion of the *Lysis,* where
Socrates' new-formed circle breaks up only reluctantly and
where he even suggests, plausibly, that the two boys already

1. Cf. Montaigne, *Essays* "On Friendship."

think of him as a friend, is clear evidence of this ability. By alleging, then, a failure to acquire a friend, Socrates must mean instead that he has not yet found anyone, even among his friends, whom he can call a friend in the strictest sense of the word. We do not yet know what difficulties he has in mind, but whatever they are, it is perhaps easier for him to discuss them with Lysis and Menexenus than it would have been with his closer companions.

Lysis and Menexenus, in addition to being friends, are probably the two youngest interlocutors of Plato's Socrates. Their age helps to explain what might otherwise appear to be a serious omission from the dialogue. For there is no reference in it to the durability which is ordinarily said to distinguish true from casual friendship or from merely sexual love.[2] In particular, the *Lysis* contains no mention of trust *(pistis)*. The dialogue may be contrasted in this regard with Aristotle's more customary analysis in the *Eudemian Ethics.* Aristotle observes there that stability marks off the highest from the lower forms of friendship and that stability depends upon the growth of reciprocal trust.[3] Now Plato is of course aware of the importance of stability in friendship and of trust as its foundation. So-called "pledges of trust" *(pisteis)* play a central role in the second highest friendship discussed by Socrates in the *Phaedrus* (256d1). Yet the question of trust is not addressed directly in the *Lysis,* and this must be in part because of the youth of the two boys. Since they can not yet know much

2. "Love as desire aims at the now. It wants to drink in the moment for the sake of the moment it swears will last. Its eternity is the moment. . . . Friendship, however, wants to last." Kurt Riezler, *Man, Mutable and Immutable: The Fundamental Structure of Social Life* (Chicago, 1950), p. 198.

3. Aristotle *Eudemian Ethics* 1237b8–14; cf. *Nicomachean Ethics* 1156b29, and Cicero *De Amicitia* 65, xviii.

about those circumstances in life which make trustworthy friends difficult to find, there is no reason for Socrates to raise the question with them. Yet this dramatic situation, and Socrates' consequent silence about trust, may turn out to contribute to the truth of the discussion. For among other things, had Socrates praised the trustworthiness of true friends, we would have been tempted to forget that no human being—however reliable—can pledge to remain alive. If only because men are mortal, no man can give another the security which he may desire in friendship. Whatever else a human friend may be, he is not someone in whom a wise man would place unlimited trust.[4]

4. "*Das gemeine Menschenschicksal, an welchem wir alle zu tragen haben. . . . Wir mögen unter dem Schutz von Eltern und Verwandten emporkommen, wir mögen uns an Geschwister und Freunde anlehnen, durch Bekannte unterhalten, durch geliebte Personen beglückt werden, so ist doch immer das Final, dass der Mensch auf sich zurückgewiesen wird, und es scheint, es habe sogar die Gottheit sich so zu dem Menschen gestellt, dass sie dessen Ehrfurcht, Zutrauen und Liebe nicht immer, wenigstens nicht gerade im dringenden Augenblick, erwidern kann.*" Goethe, *Aus meinem Leben: Dichtung und Wahrheit*, Book 15 (Munich: Goldmanns Gelbe Taschenbücher, 1962), p. 185. ["The common destiny of man, which we all have to bear. . . . We may grow up under the protection of parents and relatives, we may find support from brothers and sisters and friends, we may be entertained by acquaintances and made happy by beloved persons. But still, the finale is always that man is thrown back upon himself, and it seems as if even the Deity had taken such a position toward man so as not always to be able to respond to his reverence, trust, and love—at least not precisely in the moment of urgency."]

Socrates' Meeting
with Hippothales
(203a1–207d4)

Socrates' Meeting with Lysis' Lover Hippothales and His Group, and His Approach to Lysis and His Friend Menexenus: A Look at Community among Lovers and Friends, and Its Relation to Self-regard

Socrates narrates to a nameless audience of one or more the story of an encounter and conversation he once had with some Athenian boys. We do not know when or why he chose to recount his experience. Yet the very reporting of this friendly talk indicates Socrates' aversion to friendships based on secrecy or on the exclusion of all outsiders.

Socrates begins by saying that he was making his way from the Academy straight to the Lyceum along the road just outside the city wall. As he approached the spring of Panops, the "all-seeing," he happened to meet a group of youths standing around. Two of these boys, Hippothales and Ctesippus, were known to him by name. Hippothales, who knew Socrates as well, greeted him with the usual questions of where he had been and where he was going. Socrates' reply is somewhat brusque. He tells the boys that he is going directly to the Lyceum. Unimpressed by Socrates' apparent hurry to be on his way, Hippothales tells him to come instead directly to his

group. He asks Socrates why he won't stop in, and he adds
that it would be worth his while to do so. Socrates is not convinced, but he is curious enough to ask who belongs to Hippothales' group. Hippothales responds by mentioning that inside a nearby enclosure there are quite a few other boys—and
good-looking ones, too. Socrates now shows an increased
curiosity. He seems more attracted by unknown boys who are
said to be beautiful than by acquaintances who may not be
outstanding in beauty or in any other way.

Socrates wants to know in particular what the enclosure is
and how the boys spend their time there. Hippothales replies
that it is a newly built wrestling school, where, however, they
give most of their time to discussion. He adds that they would
be glad to share their discussions with Socrates. Socrates
thanks him for his generous offer, but he still hesitates to
enter. Fearing, perhaps, that the boys' teacher might regard
his presence as an intrusion, he asks who the teacher is. Hippothales replies that he is a man named Miccus ("small"),
whom he calls a companion of Socrates and who, he says, also
praises Socrates. Socrates in turn praises Miccus. Swearing by
Zeus, he calls him a capable sophist, or teacher. And so Hippothales, renewing his request, asks Socrates whether he
would like to enter and see those who are inside.

We observe that Hippothales' offer to Socrates is twofold—
to share in speech with him and to show him good-looking
boys. Now this offer is of course meant to be attractive to
Socrates in particular. But beyond that, friendship might be
more possible among those who enjoy speech and who enjoy
looking at beauty than it is among others. For these pleasures,
while they may exist in solitude,[1] are not diminished but

1. Cf. *Theaetetus* 189e4–190a2.

rather often enhanced through sharing. Hippothales' generous offer, however, and the boys' promised beauty are not enough to turn Socrates from his previous intention. He says that first he would be glad to learn—that is, he will not go in until he learns—on what terms he is to enter and who the (most) beautiful boy is. At least the first part of Socrates' request suggests an awareness that Hippothales and others may have private motives even for such common activities as the sharing in conversation. He therefore hesitates to accept an apparent favor which might in fact be intended as a tacit exchange for some future service.[2] The second half of Socrates' question points to the fact that the beautiful may be for some a source of discord rather than community. For not only are there the conflicts arising from disagreement about what is beautiful,[3] but even where the perception is common, men may quarrel from a desire each to possess as his own the beauty they behold.[4] Beauty guarantees friendly sharing as little as does speech.

In response to Socrates, Hippothales is silent about why he wants his company, and he refuses to name a single (most) beautiful boy. Each of us has a different opinion about that, he says. He neither claims to know nor does he admit not to know. It looks instead as if he believes, with Protagoras, that what seems beautiful to each is so in truth for him.[5] This complacent acknowledgment of different opinions undermines the friendly notion of a shared perception of the beautiful. At the same time, however, it attempts to lessen the danger of dispute. But when pressed by Socrates to say whom *he* considers most beautiful, Hippothales blushes. By eliciting this blush,

2. Cf. Aristotle *Nicomachean Ethics* 1162b31–1163a9.
3. Cf. *Euthyphro* 7e1–5.
4. Cf. Xenophon *Memorabilia* II 6.21.
5. Cf. *Theaetetus* 152a6–8; 172a1–4.

Socrates shows that Hippothales does not in fact believe that everything which seems beautiful is so for him and only for him who thinks it so. In his heart he passionately believes to know who is beautiful in an unqualified way. As Socrates easily surmises, this is because he is in love and even far gone in love. Hippothales' blush tells us both that he is in love with someone and that he is ashamed to reveal this love to Socrates. Both his love and his sense of shame reveal more about him than did the opinion which he first uttered and behind which he had tried to hide.

By this time Socrates may have guessed the motive for Hippothales' invitation. He asserts that for the most part he is inferior and useless, but that a god has somehow given him the one gift of quickly being able to recognize a lover and a beloved. This oblique reference to Socrates' divine gift causes Hippothales to blush even more. For not only the fact of his love but also the identity of his beloved could be discovered by such a keen-sighted man. Socrates is surely correct in suggesting that his divine gift makes him useful to some extent. For he could tell a lover like Hippothales whether or not his beloved loves him in return. Yet Socrates' gift does not compel him to make his knowledge available to others unless he thinks that the time is right (cf. 222a6-7).

After Hippothales' second blush, Ctesippus becomes indignant at all this sudden modesty. How charming, he tells his comrade, that you blush before Socrates and shrink from mentioning the name of your favorite! Ctesippus then turns to Socrates and tells him that if he were to spend only a little time with Hippothales, he would be worn out listening to him. Ctesippus seems to feel slighted by Hippothales, and so he tattles on him. He not only tells Socrates the name of Lysis, but he lets out that Hippothales sometimes drinks too much and that he then talks unceasingly of his favorite. He adds that Hippothales sounds terrible when he talks about Lysis, and that he composes poems and writings about him which are still more terrible than the rest of his speech. Worst of all is the fact that he sings of his beloved in an "amazing" voice, whose cacophony his companions must endure. And yet this boy, who is usually so shameless in speaking of his love, blushes in response to Socrates' questions! Socrates, of course, does not think of blaming Hippothales for the tasteless behavior about which he has been told.

Here, let us step back for a moment and look at the relationship between Hippothales and Ctesippus. Though they are clearly companions who spend much of their time together, they are never spoken of as friends by Socrates or by anyone else in the dialogue. This fact may be a mere accident, but perhaps also it is because they are not so much friends as members of a group. Their companionship is less a close tie between individuals than an attachment that binds each one indefinitely to the others in his group. Plato even points to this aspect of their comradeship by having Socrates once refer to Ctesippus with a plural pronoun (206c6; cf. 204c7 and 205d4). We see in Hippothales' preoccupation with Lysis, and in Ctesippus' resentment of his deference to Socrates, the typical weaknesses of such a circle of "friends." As members of such a group, men try to satisfy both their desire to share love and their desire for honor or respect. Yet while attempting to satisfy both of these desires in the same community, they are generally unable to fulfill either adequately. For some, this lack within the group comes to light through the experience of passionate love. These lovers become, like Hippothales, somewhat oblivious of their companions. More commonly, however, men are in the position of Ctesippus. Their desire for honor is not sufficiently satisfied by their being a part of a circle. Thus, jealousy is awakened when they see one of their companions honoring another, and especially an outsider, more highly than themselves. Both the desire for honor and the desire for love lead a man to be discontented with his place in his immediate circle. As a result, circles of friends—including political communities of "free and equal" friends—are always threatened with discord and with disintegration.

To return to the text, we note that Socrates ignores the ill will between the two youths and asks instead about Lysis. He assumes that Lysis is young, for he does not recognize the boy's name. Ctesippus accounts for Socrates' ignorance by explaining that Lysis is still called by his patronymic, inasmuch as his father is a well-known man. Lysis still lives in the shadow of his father. But he can be distinguished from all others by his looks alone, and Ctesippus has no doubt that Socrates has noticed this youthful beauty. Socrates then asks whose son he is. It turns out that Socrates does in fact know Lysis by his patronymic—son of Democrates—and on learning who he is, he exclaims to Hippothales that he has discovered a noble and dashing love. And now for the first time Socrates admits to having some human knowledge in addition to his divine gift. He suggests a competence in erotic speechmaking. He asks Hippothales for a display of his speeches, so that he may see if he knows how a lover should speak about his favorite to him or to others. Socrates seems to assume that the same things should be said of one's beloved in public and in private. Yet in his case, this assumption is not so much shamelessness as it is a sign that he would say nothing in private to his favorites that he need be ashamed for others to hear.

Instead of giving Socrates the requested display, Hippothales objects that he has not written any love poetry. Apparently his songs are spontaneous or from the heart. Ctesippus calls his denial crazy, but none of this matters to Socrates. He does not care about any particular verses or tunes, be they written or otherwise. Instead, he wants to know the underlying thought or intention with which Hippothales approaches his beloved. At this point Hippothales observes sarcastically that Ctesippus will tell Socrates what he wants to hear; for he must remember perfectly if, as he alleges, he has been talked deaf hearing about Lysis. Hippothales may still be ashamed to bare his own soul before Socrates.

Ctesippus does in fact have a strikingly good recollection of Hippothales' love verses. He claims that they are ridiculous, for despite Hippothales' special attention to Lysis, he has found nothing private to say. This apparent failure to achieve intimacy seems to Ctesippus ridiculous in a lover. Instead of speaking from private knowledge, Hippothales merely repeats what the whole city sings about Lysis' ancestors, about their wealth, their horse-breeding, and their victories at the games. Some of the poems are even more old-fashioned than these, and they remind Ctesippus of the songs of old women. For example, just the other day Hippothales composed a poem about a feast which was said to have been given to Heracles by one of Lysis' ancestors, the ancestor being himself a son of Zeus. Ctesippus concludes by saying that he and his companions are compelled to listen to all these songs and speeches.

Socrates agrees with Ctesippus that Hippothales is ridiculous, but he thinks so for a different reason. According to him Hippothales is ridiculous for having composed and sung praises of himself before being victorious in his pursuit of Lysis. Hippothales, however, appears to be too much in love to be concerned with ridicule or, more generally, with his reputation. He does not mind being called ridiculous; he objects rather to the suggestion that his praise of Lysis is in fact praise of himself. Hippothales resents the imputation that he is selfish or self-regarding. His love brings in its wake forgetfulness of self and gives him the sense that he cares more for his beloved than for himself. Socrates, however, shows him that the songs are indeed praise of himself, for the more highly Hippothales praises Lysis, the more this will redound to his own credit if—as he hopes—he catches the boy. If, on the other hand, the boy should escape him, Hippothales will seem ridiculous, and the more highly he has praised the greater will be the beautiful and good things he'll have been deprived of. It would appear from Socrates' account that Hippothales accepts present ridicule in large measure because he hopes for future praise. Like any love-poet, Hippothales is not wholly impervious to the desire for high regard and even the high regard of those other than his beloved.

If we look more closely at Socrates' speech, we note with some surprise that he does not say that greater praise of the beloved leads to greater ridicule if he escapes, but rather that it leads to greater loss. Though Socrates may well be concerned about the danger of ridicule, he also pays attention to other dangers. What most concerns him, apparently, is that greater praise breeds greater hopes in the lover who praises, whether or not this praise is deserved by the beloved. And the loss of these fair hopes may well be as painful as that of any other beautiful and good things. Socrates continues this thought by warning Hippothales that whoever is wise in erotic matters does not praise his beloved before he catches him, since he fears how the future may turn out. It is worth noting that Socrates does not limit the wise lover's fear to fear of failure in his pursuit. For even an honored, successful suitor may be pained to discover that his beloved is not so good, and does not bring him such happiness, as he had hoped. And since the beautiful, in a lover's eyes, is at least in part "the promise of happiness," or of good to himself,[6] such a discovery might well cause the beloved to appear less beautiful than before. A suitor's sincere praise, then, is always foolish, since only experience can tell how good, and therefore in a sense how beautiful, is the object of his longing.

Although Socrates has now exposed the self-regarding aspect of Hippothales' praises, he has in no way blamed him for this. In fact, he has even advised Hippothales how he might pursue his love more wisely. And now he becomes still more pedestrian. He observes that praise tends to fill the beautiful ones with high thoughts and bragging. Hippothales hesitates a bit to agree that this makes them harder to catch, but he is sure that a lover who scares away his beloved is not much of a hunter. He also agrees that one whose speeches and songs make their hearer savage, instead of beguiling him, is a poor musician. We note that this last conclusion would hold whether or not one has "caught" the beloved. In particular, such a hunter or such a musician defeats his own purpose. Here Socrates rightly surmises that Hippothales would not be willing to agree—with Socrates?—that a man who harms himself through his poetry can be a good poet. Hippothales has already shown, when he presented his love-songs as spontaneous and not composed (compare 205a5–6 with 205d7), that he cared for a reputation as a good poet. But now he is led to admit as his opinion that the end by which poetry should be judged is, or at least must include, the advantage of the poet himself. He is not so crazy or self-forgetful as to neglect to consider his own good.

6. Cf. *Symposium* 204d5–e7.

Socrates has gradually stripped the veil of total selflessness from Hippothales' love. He has shown him to be concerned with being praised as the "captor" of a beautiful youth and as a good love-poet as well. Furthermore, he indicates that Hippothales' most pressing wish is to capture, for himself, the "beautiful and good" Lysis. Yet Socrates brings all this so gracefully to light that Hippothales feels free now to speak of the self-interested motive behind his original offer to share speeches with him. He hopes that Socrates will advise him what one should say or how one should act in order to endear oneself to one's favorite. Socrates does not hesitate to offer his help. But though Hippothales had asked what "someone" should say or do to endear oneself to one's favorite, Socrates' response points to the limited usefulness of all such universal rules. Any universal maxims which Socrates might know (cf. 210e2–5) are inadequate as guides for action unless accompanied by an application of his skill to the particular circumstance. Only in conversation with Lysis in particular could Socrates perhaps show Hippothales how to speak to him. Socrates says nothing about the difficulty which a boy might have in imitating a grown man's way of speaking. And he is silent about that aspect of Hippothales' request which was for advice on how to act—rather than what to say—in order to endear oneself to one's favorite. Yet to initiate a face-to-face conversation with Lysis is itself an action.

Hippothales is quite willing to allow Socrates to demonstrate on his beloved. He appears confident that there is no danger of Lysis' falling in love with Socrates. He explains that it will be easy for Socrates to bring Lysis into a conversation if he enters the wrestling school, sits down, and begins conversing with Ctesippus. Lysis, he observes, is unusually fond of listening, and because of the holiday he is allowed to be

together with the older youths. Hippothales implies that Lysis
would have stayed away, as the law required, on any other
day. If Lysis happens not to come, however, Hippothales tells
Socrates to let Ctesippus call him, for they are acquainted
through Lysis' closest companion, Menexenus. Lysis is apparently a compliant fellow, though he might be too bashful
to come if called by Socrates himself.

Following Hippothales' advice, Socrates entered the wrestling school along with Ctesippus. There they found that the
boys had offered a sacrifice and pretty much finished with the
sacred victims. We may assume that they had eaten a meal and
were comfortable as a result. (Friendship is not appropriately
discussed in an atmosphere of austerity.) Most of the boys
were playing outside, but some of them were playing odds
and evens with dice in the corner of the dressing-room. A
number of boys, including Lysis, were standing around and
watching this latter group. These spectators would, of course,
keep their holiday clothes the cleanest. Lysis was wearing a
wreath, and Socrates could tell even from his looks that he
was worthy to be called not only beautiful, but even beautiful
and good. Socrates and Ctesippus went to the opposite corner
of the dressing room, in order to escape from the noise of boys
playing, and they began to converse about something or
other.

At this point it became clear to Socrates that Lysis was not
self-sufficient or wholly happy, for he looked around frequently, obviously desiring to know what was being said. But
cherishing the appearance of contentment with himself, Lysis
tried to conceal his curiosity, and he stayed for a while where
he was. Socrates was in no hurry to help him out of his im-
passe by having Ctesippus ask him to come over. After a
while, however, Menexenus came in from playing outside and

sat down beside Socrates without any hesitation. Lysis then came over and sat down himself, making it appear that he was only joining his closest friend. He used the decent pretext of visiting his friend in order to come to know the stranger who attracted him. The other boys followed behind Lysis. In particular, there came the lover Hippothales, who remained standing and who carefully concealed himself from Lysis' view, fearing lest he might incur the hatred of his beloved.

Instead of speaking to Lysis, Socrates made him wait a while longer by addressing his friend Menexenus. Since these two boys are closest friends, their relationship must appear to be more perfect than the tenuous bond between Hippothales, Ctesippus, and their other comrades. Yet Socrates' initial questions show that even this friendship is marked by the spirit of rivalry which had characterized the others. To be sure, the boys' competitiveness may be for the most part a source of friendly pleasure, rather than a simple barrier to their friendship. But even if it should not get out of hand, it is still at variance with the desire for union or for sharing with a friend. The high degree of rivalry between Lysis and Menexenus appears at once, for when asked which of the two is older, Menexenus replies that they dispute about it. It would have been easy for him to say that they are the same or almost the same age. But even these closest friends, it seems, do not willingly give up the sense of their own superiority. Socrates thereupon surmises that there would also be strife over which of the two is nobler, that is to say, of the more distinguished family.[7] Menexenus agrees that there is indeed a great deal of strife between them over this. Socrates then adds that there would presumably also be strife over who is the more beau-

7. Cf. *Protagoras* 337a6–b3.

tiful. Lysis cannot keep silent at this, and both boys together laugh. This shared laughter points to some measure of agreement. For these young boys are likely to agree that a competition in beauty would be silly and an embarrassment to them. Yet concealed within their common laughter there may also be a difference between the boys. For we assume, in part from everyone's silence about Menexenus' appearance, that Lysis is manifestly the better looking of the two. He might, then, be unkind enough to laugh—not only at the odd question—but at his friend's relative ugliness as well. At all events, what is perhaps most important about these first three topics is that age, nobility of birth, and beauty, while they may be equal between friends, cannot be shared with them.

Socrates next turns his attention to something that can be shared. He says that he will not ask which of the boys is wealthier, since they are friends. The two boys agree emphatically that they are friends, and so Socrates concludes that in that case they will not differ in wealth, for the things of friends are said to be in common. The willingness to share their wealth, both now and in the future, is a test of whether the boys speak truly in calling themselves friends. Lysis and Menexenus, being young and generous, agree as a matter of course that they can each be counted on to help the other in this respect.

At this point in the conversation, Menexenus was called away, apparently to take care of something concerning the sacrifices. Socrates was thus prevented from asking which of the two boys was juster and wiser. From Socrates' juxtaposition of justice and wisdom it looks as if the same boy would be thought to excel in both these virtues. Perhaps this is in part because justice includes helping one's friends, and the wise man would be best able to do this (cf. 209c2–210d4). Perhaps also Socrates would have gone on to suggest a friendlier and better direction for the boys' spirit of rivalry; they could compete in wisdom and in being the juster or more generous friend, and in this competition even the loser could hardly have complained.[8] But beyond this, justice and wisdom—at least in some of their aspects—can be taught and thus shared with others. They can be shared, in fact, more genuinely than wealth, and a man can impart them to others without any loss of his own portion. On several grounds, then, the pursuit of justice and wisdom seems to be in harmony with friendship. It appears to offer to those who engage in it a way out of the conflict between self-regard and the desire for community among friends. Yet it remains to be seen, especially in the case of wisdom, to what extent this appearance is justified.

8. Cf. Aristotle *Nicomachean Ethics* 1162b6–13.

Socrates' Conversation
with Lysis
(207d5–210d8)

Socrates' Argument That Everyone Will Befriend the Wise Man, and Him Alone, Because Only the Wise Are Useful and Good

Socrates' speech with Lysis culminates in the agreement that Lysis is not wise and that he must become wise if he wishes to be free, to be a ruler, and to be loved. This Socratic argument serves both broader and narrower purposes. Considered narrowly, it is an answer to Hippothales' request for advice as to how one could become dear to his favorite. Socrates has already faulted Hippothales for praising Lysis and filling him with proud thoughts. Hippothales in turn admitted that it was at least likely for such a boy, when filled with proud thoughts, to become harder to catch. This view might seem to imply that the best way to win Lysis' love is to humble him instead. And Socrates later suggests that his speech served as just such a humbling. To be sure, he never even claims that Hippothales could have won Lysis' affection merely by humbling him. But such an action might nevertheless be a necessary first step toward his end. Before Lysis can become a lover of Hippothales—before, in fact, he can conceive any new love—he must be freed from the belief in his own self-

83

sufficiency (cf. 215a7–b3). More precisely, he must be freed from the belief that his wants are, and will continue to be, provided for. He must be led to question the vain assumption that he already has all the friends he needs.

It is possible, of course, that once awakened to his own desires, Lysis will conceive some desire quite different from a love for Hippothales. In fact, Socrates' speech appeals to a global ambition whose satisfaction might even be hindered by excessive love for any one human being. But this does not mean that Socrates has broken his agreement to help Hippothales. For in the first place, Socrates interprets their agreement more broadly than does Hippothales. While Hippothales wanted to know how to win Lysis' affection, Socrates offered instead to show how one should speak to him. He left undetermined the end or ends of such proper speaking. (Contrast 206c5–6 and 205a1–2 with 206c2–3.) Moreover, despite the greater breadth of Socrates' concerns, his speech does not entirely neglect Hippothales' love. If Hippothales is a genuine lover, he wants Lysis to be happy (cf. 207d5–8). And Socrates does advise Lysis how to become happy. Even, then, if Lysis' happiness should not include a love for Hippothales, how can his lover justly complain? A further connection with Hippothales' interest follows from the fact that Socrates advises Lysis how to become more lovable, or more useful to others. And whether or not this makes him easier for Hippothales to catch, it may be indispensable counsel if he is to become a catch worth keeping.

To see Socrates' speech in its proper context, it helps also to consider the opinion against which it is chiefly directed. We already indicated that Socrates challenges the false self-satisfaction and contentment that come to Lysis from his present friendships. The dialogue has prepared us for this somewhat by pointing to flaws even in such close friendship as that between Lysis and Menexenus. But the attachments which mean most to Lysis and which most comfort him are not those uniting him with his youthful friends. Like other young people, he is the recipient of one kind of friendly love which is deeper by far than the love of his friends his own age. He is loved by his parents, who care for him, who shelter him, and who would give much to see him happy. Perhaps, then, the way to happiness is to learn to remain contented with the gift of parental love. Perhaps the family is the home of true and fulfilling friendship. But this is precisely what Socrates denies. In order to awaken Lysis to his situation, he must above all free him from the belief that he is adequately cared for by his parents. And since parental care goes together with parental authority, Socrates must also question that authority, an authority which has prevented Lysis from even imagining a happiness beyond what his parents allow. Therefore, the conclusion of this conversation, which asserts that the wise man alone is loved and obeyed by everyone, is directed against the opinion that parents as parents deserve unquestioning and loving obedience from their children.

What holds true for the authority of one's parents applies all the more to that of one's grandparents and great-grandparents. Ultimately, in fact, Socrates' vision of the rule of the wise is in radical opposition to the belief that men should look up to their ancestors or the ancestral gods for guidance in how to live. Most men prefer to give the highest allegiance to, and place the greatest hopes in, their traditional gods. But if Socrates is correct that everyone, or at least everyone aware of his own best interest, will accept Lysis' rule once he becomes wise, it must be assumed that men are not yet adequately ruled or cared for by anyone. This is the assumption on the basis of which Socrates opposes the customary exhortation toward pious obedience. A sign of this is that the conversation we are examining occupies the time during which Menexenus is away to perform his pious duty.

It has been necessary to dwell on the "subversive" element in Socrates' approach to Lysis, for Socrates himself never speaks explicitly of this aspect of his design. What occurs to him to say at the end of this section is, rather, that he has spoken properly to Lysis by humbling him and drawing in his sails. Now the demonstration of our great ignorance is indeed a central feature of Socrates' introduction to philosophy, but this alone would be insufficient if he did not also encourage a bit the rebelliousness which lies dormant even in well-mannered young boys. Therefore, Socratic education could look from the parents' point of view like corruption of the young. Indeed, it would be so except for the fact that he is not introducing his hearers to idle pleasures, but to the pursuit of wisdom and true virtue. Socratic education is not so much a war against parents as it is an attempt to make the young worthy of their parents' love.

To begin his conversation, Socrates addresses Lysis by his own name and asks him if his parents love him very much. Lysis replies that they do indeed. It follows as a matter of course that they wish him to be as happy as possible. Lysis further agrees that no one is happy if he is a slave and unable to do what he wants. The notion that happiness is equivalent to the freedom to do whatever one wants characterizes young Lysis as already moulded by the democratic regime in which he lives.[1] In accordance with Lysis' understanding, then, it

---

1. Cf. *Republic* 557b; 561d; *Laches* 179a4–8; also Aristotle *Politics* 1310a32–35.

seems that his parents would try to promote his happiness as eagerly as possible, by allowing him at the very least to do what he wants. But Lysis swears that his parents prevent him from doing many things. Here Socrates wonders how this behavior is compatible with their wish for his happiness. He does not try to resolve this dilemma by suggesting that Lysis' parents, like the parental legislator in the *Laws* (662ff), wish him to be just or righteous as well as to be happy. Nor does Lysis ever suggest this. Perhaps this is because Athenian parents tell their sons that they want them to be happy more often than they exhort them to be just. However that may be, Socrates tries to clarify the situation with the help of a few examples. The character of these first examples is playful, and they allow Lysis to conceive in his imagination wishes which he would never dream of taking seriously at his age.

As his first example, Socrates asks if Lysis would be permitted by his parents to seize the reins of his father's chariot and guide the horses in the race for victory. Lysis swears that this would never be permitted, though he does admit that another person—a charioteer—is permitted and even paid to do so. Secondly, Socrates asks if Lysis would be entrusted by his parents with rule over the family mule team, and if he would be permitted to beat the pair of mules with a whip if he wished. The second example is clearly less exhilarating than the other, for who would choose to rule and to beat a pair of sluggish mules if he had the chance to guide instead a speeding chariot? The example of mule driving is both tamer and more cruel than the other. Yet it is in this example that Socrates first speaks explicitly of ruling, an activity whose appeal—along with that of being free—will dominate the remainder of the speech. Whatever its limitations, however, the ruling over mules is quite enough to interest the young Lysis; but it also is entrusted by his parents to another, to a muleteer who is a slave. Here Socrates suggests that Lysis must be much despised by his parents. For they show, by entrusting their property to a slave rather than to their son, and by allowing the slave to do as he pleases with it, that they value even a slave more highly than they do their son. In keeping with an earlier silence about the dangers of chariot racing, Socrates here does not mention that mule driving might be unbecoming to a boy of Lysis' station. Accordingly, Lysis might be wondering whether to be a son is no more than an especially lowly form of slavery. For while children and slaves both belong to the family, the children seem even less free than the slaves.

Socrates next paints an even bleaker picture of Lysis' situation by showing that he is not even permitted to rule over himself, that is to say over his own body (cf. 209a1). He is constantly under the supervision of his attendant, or tutor, who is himself a slave, as well as under that of his schoolmasters. Yet these further impediments to Lysis' freedom, though they may make life temporarily more burdensome, are also clear signs of his parents' genuine esteem. Lysis' father educates his son, as he does not his slaves, in order to prepare him one day to assume the responsibilities of an Athenian estate owner. His love for Lysis is such that he requires him to learn skills which are useful and becoming to a freeborn youth. Yet just as in the first two examples, here again Socrates does not refer to the beneficent aspect of Democrates' rule. Socrates evidently intends to challenge Lysis' contentment with his parents and to arouse in him the spirit of independence. From these examples Socrates concludes that Lysis' father voluntarily sets many masters and rulers over him. By insisting on the father's voluntary action, Socrates excludes the possibility that he might be acting under compulsion or from ignorance. He thus increases the temptation for Lysis to rebel in anger.

Socrates next turns Lysis' attention away from his harsh father to his mother. She, at least, he suggests, allows her son the freedom to do what he wants so that he can be blissful with her at home. As an example of such domestic bliss, Socrates asks if Lysis is permitted to touch his mother's implements of weaving. Here Lysis laughs and swears by Zeus that not only is he prevented, but also he would be beaten if he were to touch them *(tuptoimēn an ei haptoimēn)*. He is not then simply prevented from touching them. Perhaps he has come close enough to committing this offense that he has learned its punishment expressly.

At this point Socrates wonders if Lysis has earned such severe treatment by doing something unjust to one or the other of his parents. Lysis swears by Zeus that he is innocent. But if this is so, asks Socrates, in response to what do his parents prevent him so terribly from being happy and doing as he pleases? Why is he always someone's slave? Lysis has no immediate answer to this question. Socrates continues by adding that as a consequence of his slavery Lysis gains no advantage from his family's great wealth, which others control. Even his well-born body is shepherded around by others. Socrates concludes his vigorous depiction of Lysis' servitude with the claim that he rules over nothing and that he does none of the things which he desires. It is true, of course, as Socrates admits in passing, that Lysis' parents support their son, that is they provide him at the very least with food, clothing, and shelter (208e6). But it is unlikely that Lysis, especially now that he has recently finished a meal, would regard such benefits very highly. More broadly stated, Socrates, despite appearances to the contrary (cf. especially 210d4), does not seriously deny that Lysis' parents love him dearly as their very own son. But he does question whether such parental love is enough to bring him happiness worthy of a free man.

One could fear that Socrates' exaggeration of Lysis' misery might provoke him to hate his parents. Would not this be a kind of corruption of the young? But Lysis, under pressure to come up with an answer, forestalls such fears by responding that he is not yet old enough to be free and a ruler. In other words, he has not reached the age of majority. This answer, which betrays a tendency to defend his parents even when they thwart his inclinations, is characteristic of the dutiful Lysis. It is the conventional or lawful response. The law determines the age at which boys are said to be entitled to the freedoms and duties of manhood. Socrates points to the conventional aspect of Lysis' response by addressing him not with his own name, as before (207d5; 209a3), but with his patronymic. We can assume that Socrates risked this apparent attack against Lysis' parents in part because he had already surmised that the boy would not turn dangerously against them.

Socrates does not, however, rest content with Lysis' answer to the question of why his parents hold him under such a tight rein. For there are certainly some things which Lysis is not prevented from doing because of his age. There are areas in which his parents already entrust him with responsibility. When reading and writing, for example, must be done in the household, Lysis is the first one to whom they assign these tasks. On these occasions it is possible for him to write, and also to read, whichever letter he wishes first and whichever one second. A possible objection here is that Lysis' parents, who impose these tasks, are likely to insist as best they can on the order in which they want letters to be read and written. So perhaps Socrates is also thinking more generally of freedom in its relation to reading and writing. Such freedom presupposes the necessity that one read and write in an orderly way. And although this necessity is more restrictive in reading than in writing, even the reader may choose, to some extent, his own pace and his own direction. To return to Lysis, however, Socrates now reminds him of a greater liberty granted by his parents. He may, without being ordered, take up his lyre and play it. He is then permitted to tighten or loosen the strings as he wishes, and to strike them with his fingers alone or with the plectrum. Here, too, his freedom requires that the instrument be correctly tuned and well-played. But the necessity to avoid cacophony is not slavery. It does not preclude freedom, but rather even makes possible freedom in playing the lyre. This understanding of the relation between knowable necessity and doing what one wishes governs the remainder of the discussion with Lysis. Accordingly, Socrates will now avoid the phrase "doing what one desires," which had previously seemed interchangeable with "doing what one wishes" (cf. especially 207e6–7). For the remainder of the speech, Socrates speaks of "doing what one wishes" only in reference to those who are (believed to be) knowledgeable and able to choose thoughtfully how to act (cf. especially 210b3 and b7).[2]

With the help of these examples Socrates asks Lysis to indicate the cause why he is allowed some freedoms but denied others. The conventional answer that he is not yet adult does not suffice. For it fails to explain, most importantly, what it is about being grown up that gives adults certain privileges which are denied to the young. Lysis answers, with some hesitation, that he supposes it is because he knows some things

---

2. Compare *Protagoras* 340a7–b2; see also Klein, *A Commentary on Plato's "Meno,"* p. 75.

but not others. In other words, he knows how to read, write, and play the lyre, while he is incompetent to drive chariots, to govern himself or others, and to weave wool. Socrates accepts this explanation. He even rewards Lysis for his answer by calling him ō *aristē*—"you best of men." It is not because of his age that Democrates holds Lysis in check, but because of his lack of knowledge. Socrates then infers that on the very day Democrates first considers his son to be more prudent than himself, he will entrust himself and his affairs to Lysis' care. Lysis assents somewhat tentatively to this proposition, and his hesitation is not surprising. But the conclusion follows if we assume Democrates to be concerned about his own and his son's welfare and, at the same time, sensible about the means to pursue these ends. For in that case he must wish to be guided by Lysis—if he believes him wiser—rather than to guide the two of them himself and to manage their affairs less skillfully than his son would.

The argument now claims that as soon as Lysis is acknowledged by his father to be the wiser of the two, he will be placed in charge of Democrates himself and of his affairs. Not parental love alone, it seems, but that love combined with the belief that Lysis is an able man, will lead Democrates to remove the restraints he has imposed on him. Once he judges that his dear son is also a knowledgeable one, and thus useful to the family, he will provide as wide a scope as possible for Lysis to do as he wishes. Accordingly, it could seem that Lysis and his parents will then be able to fulfill their shared desire for his happiness. Such a condition might appear to Lysis as the fulfillment of all his wishes.

But Socrates does not encourage such thoughts of family happiness. Instead, he asks whether Lysis' neighbor would not also entrust to him the management of his household, if he judged him to be a more prudent manager than himself. Lysis replies that he supposes so. By this example Socrates indicates how great is the value of wisdom or skill; even a man who feels no parental love would grant to a skillful Lysis nearly as many opportunities as would his own father. We are not told explicitly whether Lysis would wish to supervise his neighbor's household, just as we were not in the case of Democrates and his household. But in both cases Lysis' silence suggests, at least, some pleasure in the thought. One even suspects that he is more pleased to imagine himself as manager of two households than of his own father's alone. For he would then have more people and more property to rule over and to do with as he wished. To see what is happening to Lysis, we recall that the argument first questioned whether his parents' love was enough to bring him happiness. It appeared that it was not, but that his parents would promote his wishes more fully once he became more knowledgeable. But the next step of the argument has led him to suppose than even a neighbor—who presumably does not love him now—might then do as much for him as his parents would. No wonder, then, that Lysis seems to forget the unique blessings of parental love and to ignore for a while any inclination he might have to confine his ambitions within the family.

Socrates continues to appeal to Lysis' ambition by asking whether the Athenians will not also entrust their affairs to him when they notice that he is sufficiently prudent. Quite possibly, this is a reference to Lysis' future sharing, as an adult Athenian, in democratic rule. At any event, there is no necessity in this example that only one man be in charge. Socrates instead leaves open the possibility that Lysis might share his tasks with others who are sufficiently prudent. And this makes sense, for if knowledge is the title for being entrusted with management, this knowledge can in principle be shared. In keeping with this, Socrates' next examples will play with the dream that he and Lysis together, if they should become wise, can travel around the world and share the pleasures of doing as they wish. The reference in this section to such shared activity may help explain why Socrates will soon address Lysis, for the only time in the dialogue, as someone dear or a friend (ō philē Lysi, 210a9).

The locus of Socrates' next examples is the court of the Great King of Persia. Socrates induces Lysis to believe that if the two of them could demonstrate to the King that they were the better cooks, he would grant them—in preference to his own eldest son and heir to the throne of Asia—the opportunity to toss whatever they wished into the boiling soup. The royal son, Socrates goes on to say, would be no freer in this sphere than is Lysis at his parents' home. But he and Lysis, he claims, would be allowed to throw even fistfuls of salt into the soup. This is a touch of Socratic slapstick. Socrates pretends that knowledgeable cooks are not bound even by the obvious standards of good cooking. He thereby gives Lysis the hope, not so much of freedom as of unlimited license—at least in the sphere of cooking. (Lysis has not noticed the full implications of Socrates' suggestion that freedom presupposes a knowledge of its necessary limits.) Yet there may be a serious point behind Socrates' comic conceit. For there is no guarantee that a man wise in some art will use his knowledge for the good of others.[3] Until now, nothing has been said of the possibility that Lysis, once entrusted with power on the grounds of some wisdom, might choose to misuse his knowledge. This was presumably not a source of concern in the ear-

3. Cf. *Republic* 333e–334a10.

lier examples, since Lysis' love for his parents and his wish to benefit from the others' continued esteem would rule out any such thoughts. But a cook for the Persian King might perhaps be excused the whim to oversalt the despot's soup; and, what is serious, he might be tempted to join a plot against him. A man trusted enough to cook the King's meals might well be in a position to attempt poisoning. Someone could object here that for this very reason the Great King would never have trusted a stranger, no matter how competent he seemed, as his cook. But this objection is answered implicitly by the next example.

If the King's son were diseased in his eyes, continues Socrates, he would allow Lysis and him—if he thought them competent physicians—to care for the boy. And here Socrates introduces another farcical scene. For he goes on to say that the King would allow them even to open the poor boy's eyes and to sprinkle ashes inside them (rather than around them). But this joke also points to a serious difficulty. The King, compelled by his beloved heir's illness and by his own ignorance of medicine, must trust someone to cure his son. It is possible, then, that he might leave his son in the hands of a quack. Or, what is also possible, the physician might use his skill to take the boy's life, just as he might kill the King if the latter were the one in ill health.[4] What this example adds to the previous one is the problem of extreme situations. In ordinary circumstances, the King would presumably not entrust a stranger with the care of his own or of his eldest son's health. Yet in a time of grave danger he would be compelled to trust the physician whom he believed most skillful. It goes without saying that a conscientious doctor would do his best to heal

4. Cf. *Republic* 333e6–8.

his patient. And it is also true that no sane man would make an attempt on the life of the despot or his heir unless he were involved in a broader conspiracy with some chance of success. But it remains true that a doctor who is known among rulers for his skill is a power to be reckoned with.

Socrates sums up his account of the imaginary journey to Persia by saying that the King would entrust to him and Lysis together all matters concerning which he thought them to be wiser than himself and his son. Lysis agrees that this is necessarily so. What Socrates means, most importantly, is that if the King were convinced of their superior wisdom in administering an empire, he would entrust to them the rule over Asia. It is true that the decision as to who is wiser rests with the King, and that his love of his own and of his family's rule might cloud his judgment as to who could govern best. Similarly, a reluctance to give Lysis supremacy over himself (and his wife) might render it unlikely that Democrates ever concede superiority to his son. Thus, the rule of the wisest would seem to be dependent upon the unlikely consent of unwise but powerful rivals. But it has already been suggested that extreme circumstances might compel a ruler to seek help and to give great power to a skillful aide or aides. To take another obvious example, events in war might compel the Persian King to entrust his fortunes to a knowledgeable general. In that case it is not unthinkable that the general could conspire successfully against the King. And on the assumption that the general is indeed wiser than the King in ruling human beings, there is little reason why his new subjects—whose interests will be better served than before—should not willingly consent to the new order. Thus we are not unprepared for Socrates' still broader conclusion that to the extent that he and Lysis become wise, everyone—Greeks and barbarians, and both men and women—will entrust their affairs to them. In these respects, continues Socrates, the two of them will do what they wish. No one will willingly obstruct them in these areas—that is, no one aware of his own best interest will do so. They will be free in these things, and they will rule over others. In this summary statement the qualification is dropped that the wise men will be placed in charge only if they are also thought to be wise by others. For while others might indeed be reluctant to acknowledge the wisdom and superiority of the wise, we have seen that this obstacle to their rule is not always insurmountable.

Socrates continues to outline for Lysis the prospect of their joint rule over the world. His interpretation of this imagined empire rests on a radical departure from the customary understanding of what it means for something to be one's own possession. What Socrates says is that all those things in regard to which they become wise will belong to them, or will be theirs (*hēmetera,* 210b5). This is so, he continues, because, they will profit from those things. By this remark Socrates suggests that the sole title to ownership is the ability to use a thing well or to one's own advantage. He is wholly silent about the legal determinations of what is one's own and what belongs to others. Apparently, Socrates arrives at this paradoxical view by reflecting on our deep, unthinking belief that our own belongings are useful or good.[5] We are attached to our possessions, which we may even call our "goods," in the belief that it is good for us to have them. Possessions which we knew to be harming us we would probably give up, since the most common reason for our keeping them is to promote our own well-being. From this Socrates concludes, first, that only

5. Cf. *Charmides* 163d2.

those possessions which truly profit us truly belong to us (210b6–c4; cf. 208e7–209a4); and more remarkably, he also concludes that everything which does in fact profit us—no matter who is the legal "owner"—is ours.[6] In the immediate context, this implies that if Lysis and Socrates become wise in everything, and if ruling wisely is a profitable activity for the ruler, then they will inherit not only Democrates' household, but the whole earth as well.

There is also, however, the other less appealing aspect to Socrates' view that wisdom is the sole title to rule and that utility is the only source of true ownership. Therefore, he warns Lysis that no one will entrust to them to do as they think best concerning those matters in which they do not become wise. Rather, everyone will obstruct them as much as they are able. These obstructions, continues Socrates, include their own parents, as well as anything which might be still more akin to them or more their own (oikeioteron, 210c2). The more intimate impediments presumably include one's own body (cf. 209a1–2 and 208c1–2) as well as one's own soul.[7] These two especially—as sources of trouble and of prosperity—we would do well to learn to govern with the mind. Socrates continues with the observation that in those matters concerning which he and Lysis are not wise, they will be subordinate to others. The things they do not know how to use will belong to others rather than to themselves. Such things will be alien property to them, for they will not derive any profit from them. Here again property is understood, with a view to its most common purpose, as that which a man

---

6. Cf. *Symposium* 205e6–7; *Charmides* 163c4–6; and *Lysis* 222c4. Compare also Leo Strauss, *Xenophon's Socratic Discourse* (Ithaca, 1970), pp. 94–97.

7. Cf. *Laws* 726a3.

knows how to use to his own advantage. Whatever of their "belongings" Socrates and Lysis do not know how to use is not truly theirs. Lysis agrees to this radical conclusion in its entirety.

Socrates has presented wisdom as the necessary and sufficient condition for owning things and for profiting from them. According to his argument, the profit to a wise man from his wisdom is twofold. First, in those matters where he is wise, he will be able to do what he wishes. That is to say, his skill will make him free knowingly to pursue what is good in those matters. Socrates' second contention is that wise men, to the extent that they are wise, will also be unimpeded rulers over everyone. Now it is hardly surprising that Socrates holds out a reward for wisdom beyond the simple freedom to act correctly. For his initial appeal was to Lysis' desire for happiness. And there is no evident necessity that a man who acts wisely in some matter will always gain profit, not to speak of happiness, from his activities.[8] Accordingly, Socrates adds that the wise will also be rulers over everyone.

Yet what is the advantage in being a ruler? Socrates' preliminary answer to this question may be surmised from the continuation of the argument. There, freedom and rule are no longer mentioned. Instead, Socrates suggests that the wise man will be a universal benefactor who is loved by everyone. But this substitution is less a change than an interpretation of what it means to rule wisely. For the wise ruler is above all a benefactor. Knowledge of how to rule is knowledge of how to benefit one's subjects.[9] And as for the rewards of ruling to the ruler, the greatest of these might well seem to Lysis to be that of being loved.

8. Cf. *Charmides* 164b7–c1.
9. Cf. *Republic* 342e6–11.

To see more clearly why a beneficent ruler would be loved by all his subjects, we must look more closely at the argument itself. Socrates' first question is whether they will be friends to anyone or whether anyone will love them in regard to those matters where they are of no benefit. Of course not, replies Lysis. Socrates then brings the implications of this argument closer to home by adding that Lysis' own father does not love him, nor does anyone else love anyone else insofar as he is useless. It does not seem so, says Lysis. Socrates then concludes that if Lysis becomes wise, everyone will be his friends and relatives, for he will be useful and good. But if he does not, adds Socrates, no one—not even his father, his mother, or his relatives—will be his friend.

The wise benefactor, then, will be loved by everyone he serves. To say this is not to reduce love entirely to love of what is useful. For Socrates tells Lysis that if he becomes wise, he will be loved as one who is "useful and good." Though it is unclear precisely what he means here by "good," he at least suggests something admirable, something beyond the merely useful. A wise ruler, for example, would be loved as one who is estimable for his skill, as well as being useful to his subjects. Why wouldn't people love such a being?

What seems strange, however, about Socrates' argument is the claim that no one will love anyone who is not useful and good. But this too makes a certain sense. For even the generosity of love, that heart of love which Socrates has chosen to disregard for the time being (cf. 208e6; 209e6–210a4; 212e7–213a3), may not be wholly separable from the lover's desire for advantage to himself. Even parents, for example, tend to hope that they will somehow live on through their children and so escape, in a sense, the evil of death.[10] It might be true,

10. Cf. *Symposium* 208b; 208e.

then, that all love depends, if only in part, on the lover's desire for some advantage.

Still, however, one could grant this much and yet object to Socrates' further claim that Lysis must become wise in order to be loved by anyone. Are there not lesser goods than wisdom which might also give support to love? To make sense of Socrates' paradox, then, let us disregard, in this context, all love except for that which is complete and with all one's heart. Now it is characteristic of one who loves to delight in and to seek to promote the happiness of his beloved (cf. 207d7). Accordingly, to love in the fullest sense would be to devote oneself entirely to serving one's beloved and to promoting his happiness. But why would anyone continue to devote himself voluntarily and without reserve to another's service unless that other were both willing and able to bring happiness to the lover himself?[11] The beloved would have to offer at least a protection against evils, for—among other things—we humans are not so self-sufficient as to disregard indefinitely our own needs. If, then, to love means to love without reserve, it would appear that no man loves another who is not wise enough and otherwise excellent enough to be of help to him should he ever be in need.

This argument is called into question, however, by Lysis' own response to it. For Lysis shows himself quite pleased to accept the love of all human beings, no matter how good or how worthless they might be. Though Socrates is known for his conviction that the wise are unwilling to rule unless compelled to do so,[12] Lysis seems eager to assume the burden of serving everyone as their ruler. It would be hard to account

11. Cf. Leibniz, *Monadology*, paragraph 90.
12. *Republic* 520a6–e5; cf. 345e2–346a1; 347b8–e2. Compare also *Lysis* 208b2–3, and p. 87 above.

for this eagerness without supposing some attachment, or returned love for them, on his part.[13] Lysis' apparent love for all human beings casts some doubt on Socrates' claim that only the wise and beneficent can be loved as friends.

Yet Lysis' response does not necessarily threaten the truth of Socrates' claim, for what Socrates means is that no one knowingly loves, in the full sense, anyone who is not useful and good. Socrates' argument, in other words, applies fully only to those who are aware, or who can be made aware, of their own best interest. In particular, it presupposes that men are sufficiently aware of the evils which afflict them that they seek to become friends of those who are good for them. Lysis, however, has been protected all his life from the most obvious evils, and he has been confident that his future life would be a happy one (cf. 208e4–209a4). The apparent source of his innocence of evil has been the shelter of his parents' love. His confidence in their love has dimmed his sense of his own neediness, of his own need for the good. And here, at the end of his conversation with Socrates, he seems to fall back into a similar situation. His hope to become universally loved blinds him to the fact that needs of his own could interfere, even if he were wise, with his loving concern for the whole human race. A doctor, for example, if he is disabled by illness, would need the services of other doctors, and he would be dissatisfied at that time with anyone who lacked the needed skill. Yet Lysis does not think of such possibilities. His confidence in being loved, and his hope of being loved in the future, make him somehow oblivious of his own needs. His confidence and his hope are barriers which hide from him his need to love, or to love above all, those who are useful and good.

13. Cf. Leo Strauss, *On Tyranny* (New York, 1963), pp. 91-93, 212.

Socrates, however, does not openly call into question the illusions which support Lysis' undiscriminating love of being loved. Instead, he uses that love in order to humble him. It was, in fact, partly with this aim in view that Socrates first encouraged Lysis to free himself, in imagination, from the limits of his family circle. For the same argument which threatened the primacy of his family subsequently threatened his confidence in his family's support. It left him exposed to the conclusion that not even his parents would love him unless he acquired wisdom.

Lysis has nothing to say in response to Socrates' remark that he must become wise in order to become loved by his parents. Apparently, he had forgotten that the reasoning which had induced him to disregard his parents also works the other way. He must now be having second thoughts. Lysis' situation is made even more difficult by the fact that Socrates now speaks to him as "you" (210c7 ff.) instead of referring, as he had done, to the two of them together as "we" (209e1–210c6). Socrates had previously fed Lysis' vanity by speaking of the two of them as a pair of potential knowers, that is, by permitting Lysis to "identify" with his more skillful interlocutor. But now Socrates pulls the rug out from underneath him. He corrects the self-forgetfulness he had induced and abandons Lysis to his own sense of ignorance. Lysis, who may have been somewhat elated, must now feel miserable. It is easy now for Socrates, by playing on words, to humble him still further by showing that he cannot be arrogant (*megalophrōn*) if he is not yet wise (*mēpō phronei*) or rather if he is still foolish (*aphrōn eti*). Lysis swears by Zeus that he does not believe himself to be arrogant. The end of Socrates' encouragement to the pursuit of wisdom is to leave Lysis with a sudden sense of his own smallness and of his want.

The Question of
Who Are Friends
(210d9–212a7)

*Transition to the Question of Who Are Friends:
Socrates' Disclosure of His Own Desire to Acquire
Friends and to Have a Good Friend*

Having finished for the time being with Lysis, Socrates
looked to Hippothales and, as he related, almost committed a
blunder. For it came over him to tell Hippothales that his conversation with Lysis had been an example of how one should
converse with one's favorite, by humbling him instead of puffing him up. Socrates held back, however, from what he was
about to say when he noticed Hippothales in agony as a result
of the conversation. (It is just possible that before restraining
himself, and thus saving himself from fault, Socrates had
already gone so far as to blurt out the name of Hippothales.)
   Hippothales' visible distress may stem in part from
Socrates' failure to leave room in the argument for the ex-
clusive love which he desires from Lysis. Yet it may also give
genuine evidence of his love for the boy. As a lover, he would
hate to see the humiliation of his beloved. And Hippothales
does seem to share in Lysis' pain; he may even be suffering
more acutely than Lysis himself. Socrates, by contrast, would
hardly have been tempted to speak to Hippothales in such

disregard of Lysis' presence if he were himself a lover of the boy. Socrates, who was not in love, exhibited to the lover Hippothales a conversation designed, among other things, to encourage one's favorite to become better and wiser. Hippothales' pained reaction indicates how difficult it is for someone in love to appreciate Socrates' "wisdom concerning erotic matters."

Meanwhile, Menexenus returned and sat down again next to Lysis. Lysis then began to whisper something to Socrates, in a manner which Socrates found very boyish and friendly. One could wonder why Lysis showed himself so affectionate toward a man who had just humbled him so. But an answer suggests itself. In Goethe's *Elective Affinities,* Ottilien writes in her diary, *"Gegen grosse Vorzüge eine andern gibt es kein Rettungsmittel als die Liebe"* (Part II, chapter 5). "Against great excellences in another there is no remedy except love." In the face of another's overwhelming excellence, one of the nobler ways of lessening the pain of feeling small is to love the source of that pain. One may even try to win for oneself the returned affection of the admired superior. Although emulation is the truer way to lessen distance between oneself and such another, loving offers the appearance, at least, of a quicker way to this same end. In keeping with Lysis' accustomed popularity, he seems to assume that it is easy to win Socrates' love. For he speaks in imperatives, as if he had some claim on him.

What Lysis directs Socrates to do is to repeat to Menexenus what he had just said to him. But Socrates is reluctant to do this. Instead, he tells Lysis to try it himself, and if he should forget anything, to ask him later as soon as they meet again. He does not arrange a definite meeting. Lysis declares emphatically that he will do as he is told. For the present, however, he tells Socrates to pass the time until they must go home by saying something else to Menexenus, so that he too may listen (cf. 206c10). Despite his earlier refusal to obey Lysis, Socrates now pretends that he must do as he commands. But he asks for Lysis' help, in case Menexenus should try to refute him. For Menexenus, he points out, is contentious (cf. 207b8–c4). Lysis agrees, adding that this is precisely why he wants Socrates to converse with him. He does not, of course, want Socrates to be made a laughing stock by Menexenus; rather, he wants Socrates to punish or chasten him. Lysis' friendliness toward Socrates may be accounted for in part by his desire to use him as a punisher of his friend.

Lysis, then, asks Socrates to punish his closest friend for the "offence" of being contentious. We now see that Lysis' friendly posture toward Socrates was not enough to eliminate the sting he must have received from their earlier conversation. He did not, of course, become angry with himself. And rather than direct his resentment against Socrates—through ridicule, for example—he turns it against his friend. In order to overcome his own humiliation, he arranges by stealth to have the returning Menexenus chastened, and not just ridiculed, in his presence. This is no mere continuation of their friendly rivalry. Lysis' action, while playful and harmless enough, contains the seeds of betrayal. Though Lysis may well be innocent in the sense of not knowing what he is doing, he is evidently not free from injustice. Seeing that this is so, incidentally, may help us to defend Socrates against an accusation which might emerge before the dialogue is over. For someone might blame him for even raising the question "what is a friend?" among these boys and for thereby threatening their innocent attachment to each other. But now we see that, on one side at least, this juvenile friendship was not innocent. We may assume that the shortcomings of their friendship would have come to light eventually with or without the intervention of Socrates.

Socrates does not openly question the appropriateness of punishing Menexenus. Though this was surely not Lysis' intention, Socrates might be thinking that the right kind of punishment is in the service of improving human beings.[1] In any event, Socrates simply says that it is not easy to punish Menexenus, since—as a pupil of Ctesippus—he inspires fear. What is more, he notes, Ctesippus himself is also present. Here again Lysis offers no assistance as an ally to Socrates. Instead, he betrays some impatience with Socrates' self-depreciation and repeats his command for him to converse with his friend. Socrates replies that he must converse, and at this point Ctesippus interrupts their whispering to ask why the two of them do not share their speeches with the others. Fortunately, Socrates finds it easy to grant Ctesippus' wish, since it is in keeping with his own intention. But he does lie about what he and Lysis had been saying in private. For he claims that Lysis—who did not understand something he had been saying—had said that he supposed Menexenus knew and had bid him to ask Menexenus instead. In truth, of course, Lysis never said he thought Menexenus knew something which he himself did not. But what he did say included an injustice to his friend. Socrates' falsehood, then, can be viewed as a friendly concealment of Lysis' fault. And for this reason there is little danger that his lie will be exposed.

Yet one part of Socrates' last remark is almost certainly true. For he does not say that Lysis confessed to not understanding something, but rather that Lysis did not understand. The former statement would have been false, since Lysis, un-

1. Cf. *Lovers* 137c13–d3.

like Menexenus (cf. 213c9; 217d1), never admits any failure in understanding Socrates' argument. But still there are such failures. In particular, Socrates' entire discussion was about friends. Yet Lysis' whispered maneuvering against Menexenus suggests that he does not understand what a friend is, or in other words, that he does not know how to treat a friend.[2] His action is itself evidence of this failure. Now as it happens, Socrates in his own way shares Lysis' ignorance of what a friend is. But unlike Lysis, he is aware of his ignorance and so wishes to escape it. Thus, after some preparation, he will devote the remainder of the conversation to an examination of the question who or what is a friend.

Socrates prefaces his questionings with an unusually intimate statement about himself. He explains that since childhood he has desired a certain possession, just as someone else desires something else. For one man desires to acquire horses, another dogs, another gold, and another honors. As for these things, Socrates claims to be easy-going, but he says that he is passionately in love when it comes to the acquisition of friends.[3] He would like to have a good friend, he adds, rather than the best quail or cock among humans, and rather than a horse or a dog. Finally, he adds that he is such a lover of companions that he would much prefer to acquire a companion than to acquire the gold of Darius, or even Darius himself.

Given the great desire which Socrates has for friends, he is naturally struck by Lysis and Menexenus. He congratulates them or calls them happy for being so quickly able to acquire this possession. We note, however, that Socrates congratu-

---

2. Cf. H. G. Gadamer, *Logos und Ergon im Platonischen 'Lysis,'* *Kleine Schriften* III (Tübingen, 1972), p. 56.

3. Compare Xenophon, *Memorabilia* II vi 28.

lates the boys not for the possession, but for being able to acquire the possession which he longs for—and this despite the fact that they have already acquired each other as friends. Apparently, then, the friendship they already have is no more than the possibility of that possession which Socrates wants to acquire. And unless they do acquire it, their incipient happiness will turn out to have been little more than a delusive promise.

But what is this possession, associated with friends, which Socrates so desires and which even friends may still lack? If the possession is something more than just a friend, why should Socrates' failure to acquire it lead him necessarily to be ignorant of how one becomes a friend of another? The most likely answer is that the possession in question is the "good friend" whom Socrates had mentioned just before (211e3–4). For we often say of those of our "friends" who prove not to be good that they were only seeming friends, and not true ones, all along.[4] In keeping with this strict demand, Socrates might well think that if someone has not found a good friend then he has not truly acquired a friend at all.

What Socrates understands by a good friend becomes somewhat clearer from his remark that he would prefer to acquire a companion than to acquire the wealth of Darius, or even Darius himself. For this means, among other things, that Darius could not become a companion—in the true sense of the word—to Socrates. Not only would Socrates dismiss all quails, cocks, horses, and dogs as possible friends, but he would also refuse to accept some human beings. In order to be a companion, or a good friend, to Socrates it does not suffice to be wealthy; one must be a better man than Darius. Only

---

4. Cf. *Republic* 334c1–335a5.

the good friend is a true friend, in Socrates' judgment, and no bad man could become a good friend. This thought is in keeping with Socrates' speech to Lysis, where it was concluded that only if Lysis becomes wise—that is, useful and good—will anyone love him or be his friend. Moreover, the suggestion that only someone wise could be a good friend provides us with at least one of the reasons for Socrates' failure to acquire one.[5]

To understand further the significance of what Socrates has disclosed, it helps to contrast the way he speaks of friends with the way that Hippothales had been speaking of Lysis. As opposed to Hippothales, who praises his beloved, Socrates first tells of his desire for friends as if it were just another desire among many (cf. 221d2–6). Apparently, he does not consider it to be of any higher rank than other men's desires for acquiring horses, dogs, gold, or honors. It is true that his erotic desire for acquiring friends is now accompanied, and to some extent governed, by the more thoughtful wish for a good friend. Yet even in wishing for a good friend, Socrates does not boast about the loftiness of his wish. Nor does he suggest that those who prefer other things to a good friend are for that reason less noble than he. What we see here, then, is a further application of Socrates' "wisdom concerning erotic matters" (cf. 206a1). Earlier, as a result of this wisdom, he had advised Hippothales not to praise his beloved before catching him. And now, he himself restrains the temptation to speak boastfully in praise of the friends he desires. He does not even praise the good friend he seeks by speaking of him as "beautiful and good" (compare 205e6; 207a2–3; and 216d2). This may be because he lacks experience of such a friend, and therefore does

5. Cf. *Apology of Socrates* 23a5–b7.

not know how great a good he might be. But perhaps also he does know the limits of what he could expect from a good friend. An indication that there may be such limits can be seen if we recall that for Socrates a good friend is, among other things, a valuable or beneficent friend (210c5–d3). But perhaps Socrates believes, as he had suggested earlier to Lysis (210a9–c5), that to need and to possess a beneficent friend is less of a good than to be free or independent.

Socrates concludes this introductory statement by telling Menexenus that he is so far from the possession which he seeks that he does not even know how one becomes a friend of another. It is, he says, because of Menexenus' experience in this matter that he wishes to question him. Socrates thus gives the appearance of seeking from Menexenus practical advice— such as Hippothales had sought from him—concerning how to win a friend. It turns out, however, that he will not ask for any such advice. Still, what he does ask—whether one becomes a friend by loving, by being loved, or by both to- gether—is indeed a form of the question how one becomes a friend of another. There is food for thought in this question even if the inquiry does not teach Socrates how to acquire a friend for himself.

Those Who Love and Those Who Are Loved as Friends
(212a8–213c9)

The Lovers and the Beloveds, or Those Who Both Love and Are Loved, as Friends: The Question of Reciprocity

Socrates begins his questioning of Menexenus by asking which one, when someone loves someone, becomes a friend of the other. Is it the one who loves, of the beloved, or the one who is loved, of the lover? Or does it not make any difference? Menexenus replies that in his opinion it does not matter. Socrates then asks whether he means that both become friends of each other if only one of them loves the other. Menexenus agrees that this is how it seems to him. This second answer may come as a surprise. For one might at first have supposed Menexenus to be saying merely that it does not matter whether the word "friend" is applied to the lover or the beloved. And this would not seem to mean that both are friends if only the one loves. Yet perhaps this consequence does indeed follow. For if it does not matter whether the lover or the beloved is called the friend, then it must make some sense to call either of them a friend. This means that each of them is somehow a friend. Apparently, then, there is some relationship between them. The beloved, if he does not love the

112

lover, may at any rate welcome his love. And so in some sense, though perhaps in different senses for each, both of them are each other's friends. Concealed behind Menexenus' disdain to become involved in an apparently small question of usage is his belief that the lover and the one he loves will, simply by virtue of his love, be friends. His first answers indicate the sanguine disposition of one who is fond of friendship and who believes that becoming a friend is easy.

After eliciting Menexenus' opinion, Socrates then asks whether it is not possible to love without being loved in return. Menexenus admits that this is possible. Socrates next asks whether it is possible for one who loves even to be hated. As an example of this, he observes that sexual lovers (*hoi erastai*) are sometimes thought to be hated by their favorites. And among these passionate lovers themselves, some suppose that they are not loved in return and some that they are even hated. Menexenus, now that this has been recalled to his attention, expresses his strong agreement. Socrates does not discuss here (contrast 222a6–7) whether the common opinion —that a lover can be hated by his favorite—is correct. Nor does he ask how often the lovers themselves are correct in supposing that their love is not returned. He limits himself to what he knows and says merely that in such a case the one loves and the other is loved. Socrates' question then becomes "which one is a friend of the other?" Is the one who loves a friend of the beloved, no matter whether he is loved in return or hated? Or is the one who is loved a friend of the lover? Or, again, is neither a friend in such a case if both do not love each other? When Menexenus replies that this last alternative seems, at any rate, to be the correct one, Socrates reminds him how far his opinion has changed. For a moment ago, his view was that both were friends if the one loved, but now it is that neither is a friend if both do not love. Now it appears, in other words, that no one is a friend unless he both loves and is loved in return.[1] Yet even this last proposition is not affirmed in its positive form by Socrates. He does not say that both will necessarily be friends if they both love each other. In the context—with its reference to those who suppose that their love is not returned—Socrates' reserve leads to the question whether friends must not also be aware of each other's love. It would seem that friendship, if it requires reciprocal loving, requires at the same time reciprocal awareness of that loving.[2] The difficulties of coming to the awareness of another's love are important in practice, but Socrates only hints at them here. For he must first consider the broader question whether it does in fact require reciprocal loving for there to be friends.

In the continuation of his argument, Socrates will take advantage of the ambiguity of the Greek word for "friend" (*philon*), which is not only a noun but also an adjective meaning "dear." Thus it might appear that he is merely playing on words, with a view, perhaps, to confusing Menexenus and stimulating his thought. But the difficulty which he raises here is in fact serious and is more probably a cause than a consequence of the verbal ambiguity. For it is strange if those who both love and are loved become friends, while mere lovers or their loved ones are "friends" in no sense of the word. How does the togetherness of loving and being loved

1. Emile Benveniste has argued that the word *philos*, in its original and Homeric sense, was consistently linked to reciprocal relations, such as those of reciprocal hospitality. The adjective *philos*, he argues, was never at first the mere equivalent of a simple possessive. *Le Vocabulaire des Institutions Indo-Européennes* (Paris, 1969), I, 335.

2. Cf. Aristotle *Nicomachean Ethics* 1155b34–1156a5; *Eudemian Ethics* 1236a14–15.

produce a friend if the two elements singly are not somehow aspects of what a friend is, and so themselves "friendly"?

To prepare his renewed questioning, Socrates restates their opinion about the need for reciprocal loving if there are to be friends. What he says is that nothing (*ouden*) which does not love in return is a friend (*philon*) to the lover. But his use, here for the first time, of the neuter gender suggests the paradoxical rendering that nothing is dear (*philon*) to a man unless it loves him in return. And if this is so, continues Socrates, there are no lovers of horses unless the horses love them in return; there are no lovers of quail, lovers of dogs, lovers of wine, or lovers of gymnastics; and there are no lovers of wisdom (*philosophoi*) unless wisdom loves them in return. Or, alternatively, there are lovers who love each of these, but these things are not dear or "friends" to them (*phila*, neuter gender). The absurdity of either consequence opens the way for Socrates' next suggestion that what is loved is dear or "friend" to the lover, whether or not it loves in return. So now it looks as if there can be "friends" even in the absence of reciprocal loving.

To prepare his suggestion that things loved are dear or "friends" to their lovers, Socrates cites some verses from the poet Solon, who happens also to have been a distinguished Athenian lawgiver. According to Socrates' (dubious) interpretation of these lines, Solon's opinion is that a man is happy if he has children, horses, dogs, and a foreign guest-friend (*xenos*) as friends. Now with the exception of the guest-friend, who was bound by ties of reciprocal hospitality, it seems possible for a man to regard these things as dear, or as his "friends," whether or not they love in return. To confirm this possibility, Socrates asks Menexenus if the poet who spoke these verses was being untruthful. The young Athenian is, not surprisingly, of the opinion that Solon spoke the truth.

For his part, Socrates neither agrees nor disagrees. His silence helps recall our attention to Solon's main thesis, as distinct from the claim—which is at best subordinate—that things loved are "friends." Solon's intention was to enumerate the constituents of prosperity. And Socrates' recent conversation with Lysis calls into question the view that children, horses, dogs, and a guest-friend are enough to make a man happy. For it appeared there that nothing, in the absence of wisdom, could bring happiness. Yet in talking with Menexenus, Socrates only skirts this question; thus he avoids for the time being a direct conflict with the Athenian lawgiver. He limits himself instead to the suggestion that the thing loved, whether or not it loves in return, is a "friend" to the lover.

As an example of such dear "friends" Socrates mentions newborn infants, who are especially at that time dearest (*philtata*) to their parents even though some do not yet love them and some even hate, whenever they are punished by their mother or their father. By this account, which Menexenus accepts, that which is loved, rather than the one who loves, is the friend. And so by analogy, continues Socrates, it is not the one who hates but the one hated who is the enemy. But this leads to the absurd consequence that many are loved by, that is, are dear or "friends" to, their enemies and are "enemies" to their friends. It would seem, for example, that parents can be enemies to their own children, who are their dearest friends. Socrates finds this conclusion unreasonable, or rather he supposes that it is even impossible to be an enemy to one's friend and a friend to one's enemy. By calling these situations unreasonable, Socrates might be suggesting that it is foolish for someone to love those who hate him or to hate those who love him. It is easier, though, to interpret his argument as a reminder that the very word "friend" seems to mean nothing less than a friend to a friend. Yet whichever way one understands this claim, we see that Socrates follows it with the stronger assertion that to be an enemy to one's friend and a friend to one's enemy is impossible. Socrates here seems to be appealing to Menexenus' experience of friendship with Lysis. No matter how widespread it might be for "friendly" love to be returned with hate, Menexenus should know that hatred has no place among genuine friends. And indeed, Menexenus agrees that Socrates seems to speak truly.

If that which is loved cannot be a friend to the lover, continues Socrates, perhaps that which loves might be a friend of the beloved. Menexenus goes along with this suggestion. By analogy, then, that which hates is an enemy of the hated. To this assertion about the enemy, Menexenus gives an uncharacteristically strong assent. And here Menexenus may indeed have sensed something important, an asymmetry between friendship and hatred. Although loving may not suffice to make a man a friend of another, the one who hates is by that fact already an enemy. Hatred is not naturally directed toward reciprocity; the hater even wishes for his enemy not to exist.[3] Whereas complete friendship among men requires reciprocal awareness of reciprocal love, concealed enmity is the most effective kind.

Socrates proceeds, however, to show the difficulties with his suggestion that what loves is a friend and that what hates is an enemy. By that account it will be necessary for them to agree, as before, that often one is a friend of something which is not a friend and often, even, of an enemy, whenever someone either loves what does not love or loves what hates. And often, they will be compelled to agree, there is an enemy of

3. Cf. Aristotle *Rhetoric* 1382a15.

what is not an enemy, or even of a friend, whenever someone either hates what does not hate or hates what loves. Menexenus agrees that this may be so. It seems to follow, then, that that which loves can no more be a friend than that which is loved.

In stating this last conclusion, however, as opposed to the similar paradox just before, Socrates does not say explicitly that it is either unreasonable or impossible. In keeping with this difference, and despite Socrates' apparent claim to the contrary (213c1), the conclusion here is not identical with the other. For the earlier one ruled out only being a friend to an enemy or an enemy to a friend. Nothing had been said, however, as to whether one could be a friend to what is not a friend or an enemy to what is not an enemy. By his silence here, then, Socrates leaves open the possibility of someone being a friend of that which is itself not a friend, or at least not a friend in the same sense. He allows that a lover might be a "friend" (*philos*) of that which does not love him in return. A philosopher, for example, might be a friend in some sense of wisdom, even though wisdom were a healthy condition or activity of the soul rather than a goddess who could love men in return. Or, alternatively, one might choose to call the sought-after wisdom dear or a "friend," in a different sense, to the philosophic lover. One could even say that both the philosopher and wisdom are each other's friends, though each one in a different sense of the word. Admittedly, this very account suggests that neither the philosopher nor wisdom would be a friend in the full sense. Perhaps, then, mere lovers and mere beloveds are "images" or "shadows" of true friends. But, to compound the difficulty, the relation between philosophers and wisdom does not seem to be an incomplete version of that friendship which involves reciprocal loving. The philosopher as philosopher does not seek to be loved. And yet the word "philosopher" (*philosophos*), along with many similar Greek words (e.g. *philoinos,* lover of wine; *philogymnastēs,* lover of exercising; 212d7), leads us to think of his as a friendly love. By his reluctance to deny the name friend (*philos*) to the lover of wisdom and to other such lovers, Socrates compels us to ask what connection there is between their loves and those which aim at reciprocal loving. If a lover of wisdom is indeed its friend, either the friend need not be a friend of a friend, or else there is some kinship between such a lover and what he loves that allows them each to be called a friend. If there is such a kinship, however, what would be its character? And how would it be related to the kinship between those friends who both love and are loved in return?

To return, however, to the simpler level that Socrates shares with Menexenus, the argument has concluded that what loves, as distinct from what is loved, is not a friend. Therefore, Socrates can ask Menexenus what they should do if neither those who love, nor those who are loved, nor those who both love and are loved will be friends. Shall they say, he asks, that there are still some others aside from these who become each other's friends? This paradoxical alternative accomplishes its immediate purpose of provoking Menexenus to admit, with an oath by Zeus, that he is quite perplexed. Yet it is, of course, a false alternative which Socrates has presented. For Socrates has never denied that those who love or those who are loved might sometimes be friends. And more importantly, he has not ruled out that those who both love and are loved might always be each other's friends—at least if they are aware of each other's love. Thus, there is no need to look for some other beings beyond those who love and those that are loved in order to find those who are friends. What Socrates has not yet provided, however, is a precise delimitation of what a friend is. He has not yet brought to light a determining principle which would include all those that are friends while excluding all those that are not. Thus, the most plausible suggestion—that friends are those who both love and are loved—has been rejected for its failure to include the entire range of friendly love. And the latter two suggestions have both been dismissed because they would compel one to count as friends some who clearly are not. It does not seem to require both loving and being loved together, nor does either alone necessarily suffice, to become a friend. Though Menexenus has barely glimpsed this, the question "Who are friends?" has opened a way to the more fundamental question "What is a friend?" (cf. 218b7 and 223b7).

Likes and Opposites
as Friends
(213d1–216b9)

Likes or Those Who Are Good as Friends (213d1–215c2)

To Menexenus' admission of utter perplexity, Socrates responds by wondering whether the manner of their inquiry might not have been entirely incorrect. Here Lysis interrupts his friend to say that it was incorrect. Or, more precisely, he begins to say this, but cuts himself short with "Yes! That's my opinion, at any rate, Socrates." By insisting that this is only his opinion, Lysis attempts to avoid responsibility for defending the view which he has just uttered (cf. 204b3). Socrates relates to his present listener(s) that Lysis blushed as he made his remark. And he further explains what he thought to be responsible for Lysis' blush—namely, that the remark had escaped him involuntarily because of the keen attention he was paying to what was being said. This keenness of attention had been manifest even from his demeanor as he was listening.

Lysis' blush shows him to be ashamed of the remark which had escaped him. For that remark, in addition to being a little unmannerly, reveals what could seem to be unbecoming seriousness over a mere quibble.[1] It is not clear precisely what is

1. Cf. *Gorgias* 484c4–486d1, especially 484c6.

121

responsible for Lysis' serious involvement with the argument. Perhaps, in consequence of his earlier humbling, he feels compelled to prove that he is not utterly foolish (cf. 210d7). Indeed, Socrates has continued to provoke such a response by the manner in which he introduced his latest questioning of Menexenus. For he began by saying that there was something Lysis did not understand, and he went on to pretend that Lysis had told him that he supposed Menexenus did understand it (211d2–4). Yet even if a desire to show his intelligence and to outdo his friend has helped to set Lysis in motion, he may still have become genuinely aware of his ignorance and puzzled by the question of who friends are. Socrates, at any rate, judges that Lysis momentarily forgot himself, and the impression he was making, as a result of his concentration on the argument. He even regards the boy's inadvertent remark as a sign of philosophy, and he is pleased accordingly. What shames the young gentleman is a source of pleasure to the philosopher.

Socrates takes advantage of this opportunity to give Menexenus a rest, and he turns to Lysis. He encourages the boy's incipient "philosophy" by not requiring him to explain precisely what was wrong with the previous inquiry. Rather, he tells Lysis that his criticism seems true to him, since if they had been examining correctly, they would not have gone so astray. And since that examination looks to Socrates like a quite difficult path, he suggests that they go back instead to the turnoff which they had passed by earlier. He is referring here to the verses from the poet Solon. Socrates now claims that they should examine the things according to the poets (*ta kata tous poiētas,* 213e5–214a1), for the poets are, as it were, their fathers and guides in wisdom. This approach to the question of who friends are is to be contrasted, in particular, with the questioning of Menexenus as one with experience of being a friend (212a7). Despite his presumed experience, Menexenus had never much reflected upon it or upon that of others whom he had heard about. He is thus at a loss when called upon to interpret his experience. The poets, by contrast, treat human experience, and the thought-provoking elusiveness of its meaning, as their theme. By so doing they are like guides (*hēgemones*) in wisdom.

There is also, however, a negative aspect to Socrates' calling the poets "fathers" and commanders (*hēgemones*) in wisdom. We saw earlier that Menexenus assumed as a matter of course, and despite Socrates' perverse interpretation of Solon's verses, that Solon was telling the truth. This unquestioning trust in the Athenian poet and lawgiver is parallel to Lysis' initial reliance on his parents' "wisdom" and love. The poets are themselves ancestral authorities who, to a greater extent than we can easily know, have "legislated" our most comprehensive opinions.[2] Like fathers, the poets not only educate, but they also establish an authority which restricts men's horizon. Accordingly, Socrates will presently contrast these fathers in wisdom with "the wisest ones," who "converse and write about nature and the whole" (214b2-5). The wisest ones surpass the poets partly by the comprehensiveness of their theme, which is not limited to that part of the whole of immediate concern to men, and partly by their willingness to converse about the reasons for their opinions.[3] Nonetheless, the poets' very limitations help to give them a greater hold over men's hearts and minds. And indeed, it is partly for this reason that Socrates must encourage Lysis and Menexenus to follow the guidance of the poets. For were he to neglect what they say, no matter what else he discussed, he would in all likelihood

2. Cf. *Republic* 606e1-5.
3. Cf. *Phaedrus* 275d-277a.

leave untouched and unchallenged the most powerful barriers to true questioning.

Socrates' first quotation from Homer and the discussion which follows help to illustrate the poets' role in fashioning men's opinions. Socrates says that the poets speak in no inferior fashion (*ou phaulōs*) about friends, declaring their opinion of who they happen to be (214a2). Their speech is not inferior because they give a high status to friends, so much so that they say that the god himself makes them friends by leading them to each other. Socrates supports his assertion by an approximate quotation from the *Odyssey* (17.218) to the effect that a god always brings like men together. The initial emphasis here is on the connection between friendship and the divine. We know that friendship was held in unusually high esteem by the ancient Greeks.[4] And a major reason for this phenomenon may well be found in Homer himself, though not of course in the *Odyssey*, but rather in the *Iliad*, with its classic portrayal of the friendship between Achilles and Patroclus. The life of Achilles, the most admired of Greek heroes, was graced by his friendship with Patroclus, who was as dear to him as life itself (*Iliad* 18.82). For those men, then, whose taste was formed through Homer's poetry, friendship was something admirable, a characteristic of virtuous and even heroic men. Indeed, Socrates interprets the citation from the *Odyssey* to mean exactly this—that true friendship is possible only between those good men who are alike to each other on account of their virtue. This interpretation of friendship, which is still immediately accessible to us, is developed most fully in the teachings of Aristotle. Yet Socrates questions this understanding, for he cannot see what need simply good men

4. Consider the account of ancient Greek values in the chapter entitled "Of the Thousand and One Goals" in Nietzsche's *Thus Spake Zarathustra*.

could have for each other, and without anything to be gained, there is no reason for them to make much of each other or to be friends. Socrates' serious criticism here is thus akin to his critique, in the *Symposium,* of the alleged divinity of *erōs,* which cannot be a god since it stems from deficiency or need.[5] The ordinary gentleman's view is that friendship is a sign of excellence. Only noble and good men, it is held, can be true and loyal friends, for only such men are unselfish enough to wish good to their friends for the friends' own sakes.[6] Yet Socrates replies that friendship, while surely requiring some excellence from the friends, depends also upon men's wants and needs for each other; and these must be considered as defects rather than as excellences. To the Greek gentlemen, and to those many other gentlemen, who see the possession of friends as grounds for self-praise, Socrates argues that it is rather a sign of imperfection. This is the core of his criticism of Homer.

A further sign that the argument just presented forms the core of Socrates' opposition to Homer can be seen in his very quotation from the *Odyssey.* The Homeric text, as it has come down to us, is distinguished from Socrates' version by an initial word meaning "just as" (*hōs*). This word calls our attention to the preceding line, which goes, *"nun men dē mala pangkhu kakos kakon hēgēladzei."* "Now indeed most assuredly is a base man conducting a base man." These lines are spoken by the goatherd Melantheus to Odysseus, who is still disguised as a beggar, and to his escort, the swineherd Eumaeus. The "friendship" which Melantheus has in mind is a relation among low and worthless men. We are thus reminded that there is an alternative to the gentleman's posture of esteem for

5. *Symposium* 202b2–e1.
6. Cf. Aristotle *Nicomachean Ethics* 1156b9–10.

friendship. Probably the most forceful expression of this alternative is put by Herodotus into the mouth of Darius, the King of Persia. According to Herodotus, the conspirators who had assassinated the Magi engaged soon thereafter in a debate concerning the best form of government. Darius, who had been one of the conspirators, gave an argument in favor of monarchy and opposed to democracy. Part of his objection to democracy is that democracies breed strong friendships among wicked men, friendships strengthened by the friends' shared awareness of their complicity in crime.[7] Darius apparently believed that men who are exceptionally close to each other must have something to hide from the rest of the community. Now to what extent this belief is true, and to what extent it merely illustrates the despot's fear of the union of free men,[8] is not here at issue. What is clear, though, is that Socrates reminds us of an alternative to the gentleman's opinion that friendship is a sign of excellence.

To return to the quotation itself, what it asserts most simply is not that the good become friends, nor that the base do, but rather that like is attracted to like. (We note in passing that Socrates here assumes without comment that friends must both be drawn to each other, or that they must both love and be loved.) The quotation, however, does not employ the word "friends" for those so drawn to each other. And though the omission of this word was hardly of any significance to Homer's Melantheus, Socrates treats it as something noteworthy and even suggests, implicitly, a reason for it. He does this by adding to Homer's phrase, that a god brings likes together, the claim that this god also makes them acquainted. Socrates

7. Herodotus *Histories* III 82.4.
8. Cf. *Symposium* 182c3.

thus implies that if men are to be friends they must not merely be close to each other, but they must know each other as well. This may be an obvious enough truth, but such acquaintance does not in fact exist between Odysseus and Eumaeus. Rather than make them acquainted, Athena has helped Odysseus to disguise himself as a beggar, unrecognizable even by his own swineherd. Their reason for this concealment is the danger to Odysseus from Penelope's suitors. Apparently, Athena and Odysseus do not trust Eumaeus enough to tell him that the beggar he is with is his own master. For although Eumaeus has always been a faithful servant, he may not be strong or careful enough to protect such a secret.[9] By using this context to speak of the need for acquaintanceship among friends, Socrates thus supplements in advance his argument for interpreting Homer as saying that only the good can be friends to each other. For if the things of friends are indeed common (207c10), what is common must include their thoughts; friends must trust each other enough to share at least their important hidden thoughts. But no man has such trust in another unless he supposes him to be good.[10] And if only those who suppose each other to be good can regard each other as friends, then only those who are truly good will be friends in the true sense.[11]

To return again, however, to the surface of the argument, Socrates says that the poets' claim, that a god draws like to like, is the same as what the "wisest ones" say in their writings. These inquirers into nature and the whole contend, according to Socrates, that like is necessarily always a friend to

9. Compare *Odyssey* 13.405 with 16.275.

10. Cf. *Republic* 450e.

11. Cf. *Republic* 334c–335a5.

like.[12] By using the neuter rather than the masculine gender, these writers indicate that the scope of their assertion extends beyond the human, or even the animate; in keeping with this, they attribute the attraction among "friends" to eternal necessity rather than to a god. Socrates, however, disregards here the differences between these thinkers and the poets. He asks Lysis whether he has come across the writings of these wisest ones, and Lysis gives the impression, at least, that he has. To Socrates' next question, whether what they say is well said, Lysis replies with a noncommittal "perhaps." These wisest ones are not authorities to Lysis.

Socrates does not investigate the reason for Lysis' hesitancy to say yes or no. Instead, he agrees that perhaps only half of what they say is well said. For the wicked are considered to be incapable of friendship. The nearer one of them comes to another and the more he associates with him, the more hateful he is thought to become. This common opinion, which Socrates says is shared by himself and Lysis, rests on the premises that the wicked do injustice and that it is impossible for those who do and suffer injustice to be friends. And so, continues Socrates, since the wicked cannot be friends, the claim that likes are necessarily friends is not entirely true, if indeed the wicked are alike to each other. Lysis agrees with this conclusion. He might, however, had he been less well-bred or more experienced, have objected that the wicked need not injure each other. They could be like a gang of robbers, who limit their injustice to outsiders, while being just and so also friendly to each other. But Socrates would have replied that in this case, if it is possible, such men would not be wholly

12. Cf. Democritus, *Diels-Kranz* Fragment 164; Empedocles, *Diels-Kranz* Fragment 22.

wicked.[13] And his argument is directed against the wicked as such, against those who do injustice to everyone. Whether or not such beings exist in fact or in deed, thought about them allows Socrates to reject in part the view that likes must needs be friends.

Unlike Lysis, however, Socrates is not content with this easy refutation of Homer's Melantheus and of the wisest ones. Because of his respect for at least some of them, he treats them as possible authorities. This is not to say that he trusts what they say without question, but he does try to interpret their sayings in a manner compatible with the presumption that they are wisest. Since the wisest ones are likely to make sense in what they say, Socrates suggests that what they really mean by "likes" is those who are good. They must mean that those who are good are alike and are friends to each other, while the bad—as is also said about them—are never even alike to themselves, but are impulsive and unsteady (214d1; cf. 212a1; 205a3). Not only are the bad unsteady from one moment to the next, Socrates seems to suggest, but they are even at each moment divided against themselves and lacking in inner peace. And it would be hard for anyone of such inconstancy and inner discord to be a reliable friend at peace with another.[14] Lysis agrees with Socrates that in his opinion bad men are neither alike nor friends to each other. Socrates continues that in his opinion those who say that like is a friend to like are posing a riddle. The solution of this riddle is that only the one who is good is a friend, and he is a friend to the good alone, while the one who is bad never comes into true friendship either with the good or the bad. Lysis, who may be a bit

13. Cf. *Republic* 351c7–10.
14. Cf. Aristotle *Nicomachean Ethics* 1166b6–29.

abashed to learn that his criticism of the wisest ones has been premature, merely nods in silent agreement with Socrates' interpretation. But he agrees emphatically to the overall conclusion, that it is those who are good who are friends. Socrates adds his own agreement that the argument leads to this conclusion, whose importance is stressed by the fact that here alone does the dialogue speak of "true friendship." (214d7)

It might appear that even if Socrates has correctly divined what Homer thought about friendship, his interpretation of the wisest ones has been perverse. For their writings speak of nature and the whole, both living and nonliving beings; surely they did not mean that only living beings, and among these only the good, are drawn to each other as "friends." Yet Socrates could have responded that these thinkers, by seeing friendship throughout the whole, had lost sight of much of what we humans know a friend to be. For friendship involves not just nearness, but conscious love and esteem as well. But rather than so criticize his philosophic predecessors—who after all were probably not much concerned with the question what is a friend—Socrates interprets them so as to make sense in human terms. And in these terms, the understanding of friendship as based on likeness and goodness seems correct. Lysis and Menexenus, for example, are two well-born Athenians of the same age and sex.

Socrates himself, however, is bothered by something in this argument that the like and the good are friends. To explain his suspicions, he begins with a simple question. If likes are friends to each other insofar as they are alike, is it also true that they are useful to each other? To explain further why likes would not be useful, Socrates goes on to ask whether anything like would have the power to hold out any benefit to what is like, or to do it any harm, which that one could not also do itself to itself. Or could it suffer anything from its like which it could not also suffer from itself? Without waiting for the confused Lysis to reply, Socrates asks him how likes could be treasured by each other, since they would have no helpful assistance to offer. Lysis replies that this would be impossible, despite the fact that during their earlier and whispered exchange (211b7) he had refused such assistance to Socrates. Socrates does not remind him of this now, and to his next question Lysis answers that those not treasured could not be dear, or friends. So it follows that like is not a friend to like, at least not insofar as it is like.

By this argument Socrates is not denying the possibility of all affection between likes. The fact that someone capable of doing harm forbears from doing it could be itself a sign of kindness or friendliness (cf. 214e6). Yet Socrates still denies that likes, as likes, can be friends, since he is thinking, as in his earlier conversation with Lysis, of the fullest sense of the word "friend" (cf. pp. 101–102). To be a friend to another in this sense, one must be useful—whatever else one must also be—to one's friend. Still, however, one could grant this much and yet object that likes can be useful to each other without being different. There is, for example, collective strength from the alliance of many who are like each other and who are severally weak (cf. 223a5–b3 and 215d6). Yet Socrates would say of such an example that these "likes" are not so much friends of each other as of their union or of their friendship. They resemble fellow-citizens who think they love each other when in fact it is their city that they love. They themselves, by contrast, to the extent that they are all alike, have a certain "indifference" together with their "liking" for each other. For as long as there remain enough allies, it does not matter to any of them who the others are. Humanly speaking, of course, allies united in a common cause are rarely so detached from one another as in this example; but neither are they so alike. Socrates indicates something of what is lacking between "likes" by his suggestion that they would not be treasured or cherished (agapētheiē, 215a1) by one another. They might perhaps enjoy one another's company, but they would not consider one another to be valuable, let alone irreplaceable, and so they would not be friends. According to this argument, only those can be treasured as friends who offer one another something different from what they can each find in themselves.

To overcome the difficulty in understanding the good who are alike as friends, Socrates tries to defend this claim from a different angle. Perhaps the good are alike primarily in their all being good, though they are different from and valuable to each other in other respects. With this thought in mind Socrates asks whether the good could be a friend to the good insofar as he is good, rather than insofar as he is like. To this question Lysis again replies with a noncommittal "perhaps." But Socrates himself proceeds to argue that this suggestion is also wrong.

Socrates begins his criticism of the new suggestion by asking whether the good, insofar as he is good, is not self-sufficient.[15] Lysis replies that he is. Socrates continues by affirming that he who is sufficient is to that extent in want of nothing (or no one); that he who wants nothing would not treasure anything; that he who does not treasure would not love; and that he who doesn't love is not a friend. Just as likes, as likes, would not be dear or friends to each other, though they might be friends of some others, the good, as good, would not love or be friends of anyone. By this Socrates does not mean that

15. Cf. *Republic* 387d; *Menexenus* 247e.

those who are self-sufficient would necessarily not be beneficent to others. All he says is that they would not treasure or
love anyone, even though they might happen to benefit them.
According to this argument, then, one who had been benefited by a self-sufficient being might be unwise to rely on the
continuance of those benefits. After suggesting that the good
would not love at all, Socrates returns to the narrower question of whether they could be friends to one another. How
could they, he asks, since neither would they long for one another when absent—being self-sufficient even when apart—
nor would they have any use for one another when present?
What device could there be for such beings to make much of
one another? These questions suggest that the good might be
aware of one another's excellence without wanting or needing
one another and so without making much of one another.
Though they might indeed admire one another, they would
feel no desire for nearness and no attachment. Socrates concludes this argument by saying that if, as Lysis believes, those
who are good could not make much of one another, then
neither would they be friends. Lysis agrees that this is true.

   It could be objected here that Socrates has complicated the
discussion unnecessarily by considering as the good only beings who are self-sufficient. Clearly no human is good in this
sense. Even the best of men are social animals who desire the
company and need the assistance of others.[16] Socrates' demonstration would seem more appropriate to some gods than it
does to men. How, then, does it even address the question
whether or not it is the good alone among men who are one
another's friends?

   To this objection we can give a twofold response. In the

16. Cf. Aristotle *Nicomachean Ethics* 1169b17–19.

first place, Socrates is not concerned with men alone but also with truth about friends and about the good. Even if all human beings are imperfect, it makes a difference whether or not a simply good being would love. Secondly, and in more human terms, Socrates' argument compels us to consider our human friendships as a sign of neediness or imperfection as well as of our worth. It is necessary to dwell upon this simple fact, since—as has been observed already—men more commonly regard the possession of friends as a sign of their excellence alone. Someone with many friends often believes himself for that reason to be a good man.[17] And an important aspect of this belief is such a man's confidence in his self-sufficiency. For when someone is popular enough, his wants are satisfied almost imperceptibly by his friends. He typically becomes so accustomed to these satisfactions that he forgets the wants themselves (cf. 208e6). Especially, moreover, if he is young, healthy, and of a kindly disposition, he tends to lose sight of the difference between himself and his friends. He interprets his comfortable dependence as independence, and he prides himself on his "self-sufficiency."[18] Having understood himself, moreover, to be self-sufficient, he sees only generosity in his own love for his friends. His comfortable situation supports his vanity and is in turn greatly strengthened by it. This comfort and this vanity together comprise much of the charm of loving, and especially of being loved by, one's friends. Yet they obstruct the way to self-knowledge and to any such self-perfection as is possible. It is to show these obstacles as what

17. Cf. Aristotle *Nicomachean Ethics* 1155a29–30; *Rhetoric* 1371a19–21.
18. Consider the use of *hēmin* at 215b4, and compare *Alcibiades I* 104a1–c1.

they are that Socrates must insist on the fact that no beings are friends simply because they are good.[19]

Things Most Unlike and Opposite as Friends (215c3–216b9)

Since the suggestion that likes, or the good, are each other's friends has been shown to be faulty, Socrates now asks Lysis to consider where they have gone astray. Are they, he asks, somehow being entirely deceived? "How could that be?" asks Lysis. Socrates answers that he just now recalls having once heard someone say that likes and the good, far from being friends, were most hostile to one another. What is more, continues Socrates, the speaker even brought forward the poet Hesiod to testify to his position. The mention of Hesiod allows us to see that Socrates himself has been deceiving Lysis when he pretended that the poets speak with a unanimous voice (214a2–6). For now it becomes clear that the poetic tradition is itself composed of opposing elements. For this reason, above all, the authority of the poets cannot be adequate guidance in wisdom. It is, then, less the poets themselves than the strife among the poets which is the true

19. For a more thorough account of the belief in one's own goodness, as well as of its relation to Socrates' activity, see Christopher Bruell, "Socratic Politics and Self-Knowledge: An Interpretation of Plato's 'Charmides'," *Interpretation: A Journal of Political Philosophy,* 6, No. 3 (1977), 164–165, 172–173, 189–190, 193–194, 201–202, and also 197–198. See also pp. 101–102 above.

"father" of wisdom. Socrates stresses the importance of this strife by rearranging the Hesiodic text (*Works and Days,* verses 25–26) so that dissension among bards occupies the emphatic central position.

The verses from Hesiod say that potters, bards, and beggars hold grudges against each other. And in all things, continued the speaker, things most alike are of necessity most filled with envy of, love of victory over, and hatred toward each other, while things most unlike are (most) filled with friendship. We note that Hesiod's verses occur in a context which praises a certain kind of strife and distinguishes it clearly from warlike hatred. For when envy of a neighbor's wealth incites a man to work to improve his own condition, he becomes more prosperous and perhaps even more neighborly as a result. It may well be with such a thought in mind that Socrates had encouraged, by bringing to light, the emulous strife between Lysis and Menexenus (207b8–d2). Yet this very example, together with that of Ctesippus and Hippothales, makes us wonder whether rivalry might not frequently, instead of leading to hatred, be a spice to friendship.[20] Socrates does not, however, pursue this line of inquiry. This sophisticated understanding—while it may indeed suggest ways of preserving friendships among such complicated beings as men—seems of less value in the search for clarity about who first become friends and why they do so.

Even if one grants, however, the hatred between likes, this hatred is hardly a sufficient sign of friendship between unlikes. Socrates' anonymous interlocutor therefore had to continue with his argument. What he claimed is that he who is poor is

20. See Aristotle *Rhetoric* 1381b20–23.

compelled to be a friend to the rich—as is he who is weak, to the strong—for the sake of helpful assistance. Likewise, he who is sick is compelled to be a friend to the doctor, and in all things the one who does not know is compelled to treasure and to love the one who knows. Yet it is hard to see how these examples illustrate the necessary friendship of things most unlike. For if "most unlike" is equivalent to "most opposite" (cf. 215e3–216a6), not the doctor but the one who is healthy is most unlike the one who is sick. Yet despite this, it is indeed the doctor who is sought after by the sick, for he is the one they need. Moreover, there is no indication in this argument why the wealthy, strong, or knowledgeable ones must necessarily return the love of those who are deficient or in need.[21] This argument, then, seems to point less to friendship between unlikes than to a one-sided attraction based on need. This suggestion is, to be sure, an important supplement to Socrates' critique of the friendship between likes (compare, especially, 215d6 with 215a2). But Socrates' interlocutor has not yet shown how things most unlike each other are those most filled with friendship.

In order, then, to demonstrate that things most unlike are friends, the nameless speaker continued with his argument, and he did so, according to Socrates, still more magnificently than before. By the "magnificence" of this speech, Socrates may be referring to the frequent use of the causal connective *gar* (215e3; e4; e5; e9 [twice]; cf. 215d4), which makes every sentence appear like a reasoned explanation of the one before. The speaker argued that like was wholly wanting in being a friend to like, but that rather the very opposite was the

---

21. Cf. Cervantes, *Don Quixote* I xiv, in particular the speech of Marcella.

case.[22] For, he said, the most opposite is especially a friend to the most opposite. The speaker reasoned that this was so because each thing desires its opposite, and not what is like. As instances of such desire, he observed that what is dry desires the moist, what is cold the warm, what is bitter the sweet, what is sharp the dull, what is empty desires filling, and what is full emptying, just as all other things desire in the same way. There is no need for the speaker to supplement this list with the female and the male.

Socrates' interlocutor did not merely assert that opposites desire, and so are friends of, each other, but he proceeded to explain why he thought so. What is opposite, he continued, is nourishment for its opposite, since what is like would enjoy no advantage from its like. Opposites, then, are friends because they derive nourishment from each other (cf. 208e6). Yet if the friendship of opposites is for the sake of nourishment, then the opposition itself may be considered incidental. What each desires primarily is its own nourishment. A similar thought is suggested by the speaker's earlier language in referring to what is full and what is empty. For by his account what is full and what is empty do not desire each other; rather, what is full desires emptying and what is empty desires

22. The speaker's use of the phrase "the very opposite" or "the opposite itself" (*auto to enantion*, 215e3) in this context—in contrast to the succeeding "the most opposite" (*to . . . enantiōtaton*, 215e3)—suggests that he believes that only in speech or in thought can things be truly opposite to each other. One thing may be hotter or colder than another, but never simply hot or simply cold; accordingly, hot and cold things can be "most opposite" to each other, but never "the very opposite." In the same vein, the speaker's repeated use of the phrase "especially a friend" (*malista philon*, 215e4; 216a4–5; cf. 215d2–4) suggests that he believes "the friend itself" or "what is simply a friend" to exist in speech or thought alone and never quite in deed. On this last point he may be in agreement with Socrates.

filling. Had he chosen to, the speaker might have also suggested that what is dry desires not the moist but moistening, and so also with the other examples. These motions are presumably all pleasures, at least for living beings.[23] While appearing to desire or even to love each other, opposites may in fact desire to be pleased and to be nourished themselves.[24] Even where such desires happen to move both opposites at once, their desires are neither truly shared nor truly reciprocal. And to the extent that this is true, the wholeness of friendship would be a deception. The single apparent friendship would in fact consist of different "friendships." Socrates, incidentally, may have been hinting at this thought when he first asked Lysis whether they were being "somehow entirely" (holōi tini, 215c3–4) deceived. For this phrase can mean also to be deceived "by a certain whole," and friendship itself—at least to the extent that it is love of opposites—may be just this deceptive wholeness. Accordingly, when Socrates makes his own first suggestion about what a friend is, he will disregard reciprocal loving and will hardly use the word "friendship" (contrast especially 214d7 with 220b1–3; cf. 217e9; 219a4).

To return, however, to Socrates' interlocutor, Socrates concludes the recounting of his argument by saying that the man had seemed clever as he spoke, for he spoke well. Socrates asks both Lysis and Menexenus what they think of how he spoke, and Menexenus agrees that he did speak well, at least as it seems from Socrates' retelling. We do not know Lysis' opinion on this question, for here he retires from the discussion. It may be that he finds the concentration on need and desire to be uncongenial, and he might also be tired. In any event, Socrates allows Lysis' silence to pass without remark and asks

23. Cf. *Philebus* 31d4–32b5; cf. 34e13–35a4.
24. Cf. Aristotle *Nicomachean Ethics* 1159b12–23.

whether they should declare what is opposite to be especially a friend to its opposite. Menexenus, who may have also been reflecting on the contrast between his own temperament and that of Lysis (cf. 206e9–207b1 *inter alia*), agrees that this is what they should say. But Socrates raises objections at once. In the name of those all-wise men who are skilled in contradicting, he refutes and thus disciplines the contentious Menexenus (211b8–c3; cf. 216b5). These all-wise men, according to Socrates, will immediately leap upon them with pleasure, and they will ask whether hatred is not most opposite to friendship. Their "question" is, of course, not really a question, and Menexenus is compelled to agree that what they say is true. He denies, however, that what is an enemy is a friend to the friend and that what is a friend is a friend to the enemy. But as Socrates will go on to say, this denial seems to contradict the claim that opposites, as such, are friends.

This first part of the refutation might have been resisted, however, if Menexenus had observed that hatred and friendship are relations between beings, rather than beings themselves, and thus not among the opposites which are friends. Similarly, it would be misleading to speak of friends and enemies as beings which are opposites, for a friend is not a friend, nor an enemy an enemy, except in relation to another. Thus, the same being might be a friend of one and an enemy of another, but not for that reason an opposite to itself. But Socrates may have had a deeper reason for asking whether friendship is most opposite to hate. Perhaps these opposites can go together to such an extent that the same being is at the same time a friend and an enemy to the same being. We have already suggested that rivalry can coexist with friendship, and if friendship is rooted in such desire as the desire for nourishment, then it would even be itself a kind of hate. The very im-

age which Socrates uses for the all-wise men—beasts leaping
with pleasure upon their prey—reminds us that desire is not
always so far removed from hate. Just as beasts desire to kill
the prey on which they feed, the all-wise contradictors, who
are themselves empty of convictions, desire to annihilate the
convictions of others. Yet at the same time, they appear to enjoy the company of their victims. Moreover, even some higher
friendly loves may include aspects of the desire to destroy.
When parents and educators, for example, desire that the
young become better and wiser, their very love for them can
also be seen as a hatred of their present faulty condition.[25]
From these examples, then, one might be inclined to conclude
that what is an enemy could indeed be a friend to its friend or
a friend a friend to its enemy (216b2–4). Nevertheless, though
a full account of friendship—friendship with oneself as well as
with others—would have to allow for these examples, the
conclusion from them still seems wrong. The uncomplicated
response of Menexenus seems somehow right: a friend—at
least a friend in the truest sense—is neither "the enemy" nor
its friend.

This part of the refutation of Menexenus is strengthened by
an argument in which Socrates no longer clearly distinguishes
the other contradictors from himself. He asks whether what is
just is a friend to the unjust, what is moderate a friend to the
undisciplined, or what is good a friend to the bad. Menexenus
replies that in his opinion these would not be friends. Yet of
necessity they would be such, continues Socrates, if something
is a friend to its friend in accordance with opposition. Menexenus agrees that this would be necessary, and so Socrates concludes that just as what is like is not a friend to its like, neither

25. Cf. *Euthydemus* 283c5–d8.

is what is opposite a friend to its opposite. Menexenus agrees to the extent of saying that it does not seem so. The weakness of this last assent probably results in part from Menexenus' failure to see that Socrates has not ruled out all opposites as friends. His refutation applies only to the view that friends are friends "in accordance with opposition" (216b6–7). Despite appearances, he has not denied that some degree of opposition, as well as some degree of likeness, is possible and even necessary between friends.[26] But if likes in the strictest sense are not friends, and if some opposites are not friends either, then neither likes nor opposites *as such* can be friends. And since neither likeness nor opposition accounts for why friends are friends, Socrates must seek an acceptable account elsewhere.

26. See the discussion of friendship between likes and friendship between opposites, and of a third kind of friendship mixed from these two, at *Laws* 836e5–837d2.

The Intermediate as
a Friend of the Good
(216c1–221d6)

Socrates' Suggestion That What Is neither Good nor Bad Becomes a Friend of the Good (216c1–218c3)

Having shown that neither likes nor unlikes, as such, are friends, Socrates now offers an account of his own. He asks the boys to consider with him that what is truly a friend might be none of these things they have discussed. What he proposes is that whatever is neither good nor bad might become thus at some times (*houtō pote gignomenon*, 216c3) a friend of the good. Before proceeding, we note at once Socrates' most visible deviation from the previous two suggestions. Since a being of one kind is said to be a friend of one of a different, and higher kind, there is no necessary implication that this other being is also a friend. In other words, Socrates avoids the assumption, which was implicit earlier, that friendly loving need be reciprocal. This is in keeping with his recent intimations that the reciprocity among friends might be somehow a mere appearance, one which concealed the truth about what a friend is (cf. also 220a7–b3). Menexenus, however, is simply puzzled, and he asks Socrates how he intends his cryptic suggestion to be understood. But Socrates replies, with an oath, that he does not know and that he himself is really dizzy from the perplexity of the argument.

Socrates begins to explain his difficulty by adding that it may be, as the old saying goes, that what is beautiful is a friend (or "dear").[1] A friend, he continues, seems at least to be something soft, smooth, and sleek, and in this sense beautiful. Indeed, he says, this is perhaps the reason for its sliding past them and giving them the slip. Yet whatever the merits of this comparison, Socrates has not yet shown how his reference to the old saying about the beautiful helps to clarify his original suggestion that the friend becomes a friend of the good. To indicate the connection, therefore, between the two remarks he goes on to assert that what is good is beautiful. And when Menexenus agrees that he thinks so too, Socrates restates his original suggestion in the form of a divination that whatever is neither good nor bad is a friend of the beautiful and good. Since the good is assumed also to be beautiful, this new version is merely another way of saying that whatever is neither good nor bad is a friend of the good. For this same reason, moreover, Socrates can return at once to the shorter phrase "friend of the good." While not denying, but even asserting, that what is good is also beautiful, or noble, Socrates will proceed to consider it only in its aspect of being good.

Socrates' reference to the old saying that "the beautiful is dear" suggests a selfish aspect to his notion of what a friend is.[2] For "the beautiful" calls to mind the attractively new, which threatens to supercede our attachment to the old and the familiar. Moreover, although Socrates appeals to the authority of this old saying, he disagrees with it in part, and his disagreement strengthens the first impression that he thinks of

1. Cf. Theognis, 15–18; Euripides *Bacchae* 881.
2. Cf. the scholiast's comment on 216c6–7: ("a saying of those who choose the advantageous").

friendly love as something selfish. His disagreement can be seen in the following way. If we assume that the beautiful is a friend and that the good is beautiful, although it indeed follows that friendly love is of the good, there would also be friendly love of those beautiful or noble beings which did not happen to be good. (That Socrates does not regard everything beautiful as good is implied in his remark about Lysis at 207a2–3.) But Socrates implicitly denies this latter consequence. His divination that friendly love is of the beautiful and good means among other things that the beautiful, to the extent that it is not also good, will not be truly loved. (Hippothales' love of the beautiful Lysis is supported by the belief that his beloved is also good. See 205e6.) And as Socrates will indicate through his choice of examples, he understands "what is good" in this context to mean primarily what is good for the friend who loves. Although insisting that friendly love is of what is beautiful or high, Socrates refuses to separate it from the pursuit of that good which the friend has need of for himself.[3]

Socrates continues to clarify his suggestion by means of the following reasoning. He says that in his opinion there are, as it were, some three kinds—what is good, what is bad, and what is neither good nor bad. This third kind apparently includes beings that necessarily seek what is good or what seems to be good, as well as those things that are themselves indifferent to good and bad. For the sake of brevity, we shall also refer to this third kind by the Platonic term "intermediate" (*tōn metaxu ontōn*, 220d5–6).[4] Menexenus agrees with Socrates that there are these three kinds, and he seems also to accept that together they comprise everything that is. Thereupon, Socra-

3. Cf. *Republic* 607e4–6ff.
4. Cf. *Gorgias* 467e1–468a4.

tes adds that the previous argument has ruled out what is good as a friend to the good, what is bad as a friend to the bad, and what is good as a friend to the bad. If, then, he continues, anything is a friend to anything, there remains only the intermediate as a friend of the good or as a friend of what is such as it is itself. For nothing, he goes on, would become a friend to the bad. Menexenus agrees that this is true. Socrates then reminds him that they had just now said that like was not a friend to like. And on this basis, he concludes that what is such as, or like, the intermediate itself will not be its friend. Menexenus allows that this appears so, and since he accepts without question that there are indeed friends, he is compelled to agree with the conclusion that whatever is neither good nor bad becomes a friend to the good, and that alone to it alone. This, of course, is roughly Socrates' original suggestion. Yet despite the apparent rigor of the argument, Menexenus' last two responses are somewhat hesitant; he grants only the seeming necessity of Socrates' conclusion.

Menexenus' hesitation is in fact quite sensible, for there are some dubious elements in Socrates' reasoning. Most importantly, his argument for intermediates not being one another's friends is based on the questionable premise that like cannot be friend to like. Now one may grant that intermediates, insofar as they are intermediate, are like each other. Yet Socrates had never shown that likes cannot be friends, but merely that they cannot be friends insofar as they are like or insofar as they are good. That argument was enough to rule out friendship among them as long as likes were identified with the self-sufficiently good. But it no longer does so now that Socrates speaks of intermediates who, not being bad, might also be alike to each other (cf. 214c7–d3). For though intermediates would not be friends merely by being all alike intermediate, there could well be closer likenesses, combined with congenial differences, which would account for some of them becoming friends. To admit this seems, in fact, to be only common sense, for there appear to be many friendships among those who are neither good nor bad. The other social animals, for example, live in a friendly way with others of their own kind, just as human beings have friendly ties for the most part with others who are somehow alike to themselves. Accordingly, there must be a more telling reason than mere likeness for Socrates' conclusion that intermediates cannot be one another's friends. To find this reason, however, we need only recall again his early conversation with Lysis. For there he was able to persuade the boy that no human being can have friends, even within his own family, unless he becomes wise enough to be useful to them and good (cf. 210c7–d4). And Socrates has argued more recently as well that friendly love depends upon need, the need which those who are not good have for what is good (214e3–215c2). Or, as one can also say, those beings who are not good need and (if they are sensible) love whoever can help them to become good themselves. It is above all for this reason that Socrates disregards the love of those who are neither good nor bad for others who are merely like themselves in this respect.

Socrates now begins to elaborate his suggestion, and to spell out the causes of friendly love, through the use of some examples. He asks both Lysis and Menexenus whether the present argument is not guiding them in a fine way. (We note that the argument has supplanted the poets as the boys' guide in wisdom. Compare 217a3–4 with 214a1–2.) Without waiting for an answer, however, Socrates introduces his first example, the body. If, he says, they were to conceive of the healthy body, it has no want of the medical art, nor is it in want of benefit. For it is, he explains, sufficient, and so no one when he is healthy is a friend to the doctor because of his health. This argument recalls, of course, Socrates' earlier claim that a self-sufficient being would not love. In speaking of the healthy body as sufficient, Socrates disregards for the time being that even it requires food and drink to sustain its health (contrast 221a1–b3). He does this, apparently, so as not to divert attention from the far greater distress of disease. Unlike the healthy body, which may well be a mere conception of the mind (217a4–5), our bodies are all subject to disease and death. And it is serious evils such as these which compel us to subordinate the merely pleasant in food and drink to our concern for the body's good.

Socrates continues by observing that it is the one who is ill who is a friend of the doctor and because of his disease. He then shows the application of this example to his thesis. He notes, first, that disease is an evil, while the medical art is a beneficial and good thing. A body, he continues, insofar as it is a body, is neither good nor bad, and it is compelled because of disease to welcome and to love the medical art. Having gained Menexenus' agreement to all these assertions, Socrates concludes with a restatement of his thesis that whatever is neither bad nor good becomes a friend of the good, because— as he now adds—of the presence of an evil. Here, however, Menexenus again replies merely that it seems so (217b6; cf. 217a2). Perhaps because he doubts whether the soul's friendly love is likewise the result of need, he hesitates at the universal conclusion from the example of bodies. It is true, indeed, that Socrates has spoken not only of the body but also of the diseased man and of his friendliness toward the doctor (217a7). But Menexenus, who was absent throughout Socrates' early conversation with Lysis, might question whether a love which depends upon the body's need for what another knows is a sufficiently revealing example of friendly love.

Disregarding the half-heartedness of Menexenus' assent, Socrates continues with his argument. He examines in particular how the presence of an evil can cause an intermediate being to become a friend of the good. Clearly, he notes, this happens before the host itself becomes bad as a result of the evil which it has. And this is because, as Socrates adds, it would no longer, after having become bad, have any desire for or be a friend of the good. For they had declared it impossible that bad be a friend to the good. Menexenus reaffirms this impossibility. Yet Socrates suspects that the boys have not fully understood him, and so he asks them to consider what he means. What he is saying, he explains, is that some things are also themselves of such a kind as whatever is present to them, whereas other things are not. As an example he observes that if someone should rub anything with some coloring, that coloring which is rubbed on is present to that upon which it is rubbed. "Very much so," is the response. And does it follow, Socrates asks, that that upon which it is rubbed is at that time of such a kind with respect to color as that which is on it? Menexenus replies that he does not understand the question. But now, at least, he knows that he does not understand, and he is therefore more ready to learn. Menexenus' acknowledgement of ignorance is the dramatic counterpart to Socrates' assertion, soon to come, that those who still regard themselves as not knowing whatever they do not know are the ones who love wisdom (218b1–2).

To clarify his question for Menexenus, Socrates asks him what would happen if someone were to rub his blond hair with white lead. Would his hair at that time be white or would it appear so? Menexenus replies that it would appear so. Socrates then gains Menexenus' agreement that in the case being considered, whiteness would be present to his hair. But Socrates observes that his hair would nevertheless not yet be white and that although whiteness would be present, it would be neither white nor black. "That's true," replies Menexenus. Yet when old age, says Socrates, brings this same color, at that time the hair becomes of such a kind as what is present, white from the presence of white. After this preparatory reflection about being and appearance, Socrates restates his question by asking whether that to which something is present will be of such a kind as what is present. Or, as the example suggests, will the answer be either yes or no, depending on the manner in which what is present is present? At this point Menexenus understands the question well enough to agree that it depends on the manner of presence. From this Socrates concludes that whatever is neither bad nor good is sometimes, although an evil is present, not yet bad, but there are times when it has already become bad. Menexenus agrees to this, and Socrates then asserts that whenever it is not yet bad, though an evil is present, this presence makes it desire good. But when the presence makes it bad, it deprives it of the desire, at the same time as the friendship, of the good. For in this case the host is no longer intermediate but bad, and as such it is not a friend to good.

The most immediate difficulty with this part of Socrates' argument is his apparent confusion of different manners of being present with differences in duration. His example points to a distinction between naturally white hair, which is white, and artificially whitened hair, which merely appears to be white. Here the difference between being white and merely appearing so depends solely on the different manners in which white is present. It has nothing to do with how long the white has been present. In keeping with this, Socrates suggests that only if what is present is present in a certain manner will its host be itself like it (217e2–3). Yet the example of hair coloring was first introduced to help explain what it means that a being requires time to become itself bad through the presence of an evil (cf. 217b6–c3). Moreover, Socrates also concludes that the intermediate being to which an evil is present is at some times not yet bad, though at other times it has already become so (217e4–6; cf. 217b6–7 and d5). Here, as before, Socrates' claim is that the presence of evil does not make its host immediately bad, but rather leads to its becoming bad over time. But why does he use the distinction between appearing to be something and being so to help clarify the difference between not yet being something and already having become so?

An answer to this question may emerge if we consider that Socrates is concerned here above all with the presence of evil. For the corrupting effect of an evil, while it does take time, depends also and decisively on the manner of its presence. More particularly, it depends on whether or not the evil appears as such to those to whom it is present. Only when an evil is present in such a manner as to appear as an evil to the sufferer is the host not bad itself. The diseased body, for example, of a man who knows that he is ill is not simply bad itself, for in addition to harming the man it awakens his desire to be healed. Rather, what is simply bad, or harmful to a man, is that body whose disease is free of symptoms. Moreover, it also happens that a disease, though it has been acknowledged, breeds habits which sustain it and which overcome the desire to be healed. In this case, which seems uppermost on Socrates' mind (cf. 217b7–8; e8–9), the illness after a while no longer appears to the patient as an evil. We see, then, that the question of appearance is indeed related to that of how, over time, a being becomes transformed by the presence of some evil. A being to which evil is present, but which still appears to itself to be suffering from that evil, is not yet itself bad as a result of it, for it still desires and is a friend of what is good. Yet as soon as that being no longer appears to itself to be suffering from the evil, then it does not any longer even desire what is good, and it has therefore already become bad itself.

To further illustrate his thesis about the friend, Socrates suddenly introduces a much loftier example. They could, he says, assert also that those who are already wise—whether they are gods or human beings—no longer philosophize or love wisdom (*philosophein,* 218a3). Nor on the other hand, he continues, do those love wisdom who possess ignorance in such a manner as to be bad. For no one who is bad and stupid loves wisdom. The ones left, he goes on, are those who, while possessing this evil of ignorance, are not yet as a result of it senseless or stupid, but still regard themselves as not knowing whatever they do not know. It follows, according to Socrates' account, that those who are neither yet good nor bad love wisdom, but as many as are bad do not love it, nor do those who are good. To support this claim, Socrates recalls that in their previous arguments it appeared to them that what is opposite is not a friend of its opposite, nor what is like of its like. Both boys, being asked if they remember this, reply that they most certainly do. And so finally Socrates addresses the two of them by name and declares that they have discovered most certainly that which is a friend and that which is not. "For we assert—regarding the soul, and regarding the body, and everywhere—that whatever is neither bad nor good is itself, because of the presence of an evil, a friend of the good." Menexenus, who must be impressed by the example of lovers of wisdom, no longer shows any reluctance to agree with Socrates (218c2; cf. 217b6). And both boys assent emphatically to what looks to be their final conclusion about the friend.

The example of philosophizing appears, at first, as the fitting complement to that of love for the medical art. Discussion of the body would lead easily to that of the soul, which like the body is neither good not bad itself, but capable of becoming either (220c3–5; cf. 218b8). And just as the body loves the medical art because of the presence of disease, so the soul would love a good of its own, or wisdom, because of the presence of ignorance, which is its own peculiar evil.[5] Indeed, the analogy can be carried still further if we consider, instead of the being to which an evil is present, the manner of its presence. For just as bodily illness must appear to the sufferer as an evil in order for him to seek healing, so also someone suffering from ignorance must be aware of it, and aware of it as an evil, if he is to begin to philosophize. The presence of ignorance, then, makes its possessor stupid and bad only when he is blinded to its appearance and thus unwilling to seek wisdom.

An example of that ignorance which masks its own appearance is the case of someone who regards himself as knowing everything, though he knows very little.[6] There is also the seemingly different case of someone who "knows" that he knows only a little, but who believes that he does not need to learn more.[7] Yet this is in fact another instance of claiming to know what one does not know, for such a one presumably

5. Cf. *Timaeus* 86b2–4.
6. Cf. *Laws* 732a4–b2.
7. Cf. *Meno* 86b7–c2.

regards himself as knowing that his ignorance is not an evil. In other words, he regards himself as knowing sufficiently what his needs are, or what is good. Though he may not pretend to know everything, he does claim to know all he needs to know. And at least in many cases, such a man also claims to know that he is good, and capable enough to meet his other needs, or at least that he will be sufficiently cared for by others.[8] It is because of his belief that he knows what is good, if not also his belief in his own goodness, that he does not desire to learn. "For no one who doesn't suppose himself deficient desires that which he doesn't suppose himself to lack."[9] In contrast to those who are ignorant in this manner, those who are themselves neither good nor bad, and who still regard themselves as not knowing what they do not know, are the ones who philosophize. What Socrates means here, primarily, is that those who philosophize still regard themselves as not knowing who is good—for it is surely not themselves—nor what is good. Indeed, although they wish to become wise and though they do love wisdom, they do not claim to know that "the wise" and "wisdom" are more than partial answers to this twofold question of who and what is good (cf. 206a1-3).[10]

In keeping with the previous example, the presence of ignorance is not said to make its host bad all at once, but to do so over the course of time (218a7; b1-2). Here, too, the likely explanation is that our ignorance, especially our ignorance about the good, becomes harder for us to recognize as what it is the older we become. Our foolish self-love leads us as we

8. Cf. pages 101-102, 124-125, 133-135 above; See also *Apology of Socrates* 41c8-d2.

9. *Symposium* 204a1-7.

10. Cf. also *Meno* 86d3-e1; *Republic* 505a2-d1.

grow older to value ever more highly our own opinions about the just, the good, and the noble, and to be accordingly less open to what is true.[11]

But Socrates' emphasis in this passage on the temporal element has another, and stranger, aspect. Those who philosophize are contrasted not only with the already stupid, but also with those who are already wise. Socrates says that those already wise, whether they are gods or men, no longer philosophize (218a3). The temporal adverbs distinguish this statement from the similar one in the *Symposium* (204a1–2), where gods are spoken of as wise without any qualification. Whereas the *Symposium* passage leads us to think of gods as being eternally wise, Socrates is silent here about such beings. Instead, he suggests the thought that all wisdom, whether possessed by man or god, is preceded by love of wisdom. What Socrates intimates, in other words, is that no being, not even a god, is wise from the beginning or eternally wise. But how are we to understand this Socratic suggestion about the relation of wisdom to time?

Since Socrates offers no reasons here for his apparent disbelief in an original wisdom, we must sketch for ourselves what his argument might have been. If gods, he might have argued, are eternally wise, then their wisdom or knowledge must be a knowledge of what is eternal. But knowledge of this sort is not the whole of knowledge, for beings which come into being and perish are also knowable to a degree. And the knowledge of corruptible beings cannot in its entirety be an eternal knowledge.[12] This is so even though perishable beings might share in an eternal nature, which as such could be

11. Cf. *Laws* 731e3–732b4; and contrast *Charmides* 163d2–3 with 163c3–6.
12. Cf. *Parmenides* 134a3–e7.

always known, for their nature in this sense is not all that we can learn about them. To illustrate this, let us consider Socrates' own example of medical knowledge. A doctor knows not merely the nature, healthy or otherwise, of the human body. Since his knowledge is directed to action, he must also know about particular situations (cf. 206c4–7). He must know both the character of the various illnesses and the various ways in which health can be restored to his several patients. And this knowledge, like all knowledge which aims at improving the unguided course of things, is the fruit of trial and experience.[13] (Consider Socrates' reference to "experience" at 212a7.) If then, complete wisdom includes knowledge of all that is knowable, whoever is wise must have become so through learning and after having loved a wisdom which he once did not possess.[14]

This argument may be pursued further. If wisdom in the full sense is not eternal, might there not be some necessary conditions for it ever to emerge? In particular, how could a happy and eternally self-sufficient being—like the gods of Socrates' youth[15]—ever become wholly wise? A self-sufficient being, though ignorant at first of the practical arts, would not suffer from this ignorance as an evil. It would have no need of such knowledge for itself, and as Socrates has argued

---

13. Cf. Aristotle *Metaphysics* A 981a1–12; b17–25.

14. Cf. *Alcibiades I* 106d4–e3. I am here ignoring, of course, the counterargument that would begin from revealed knowledge of an all-powerful and all-knowing Creator. (See Maimonides, *The Guide of the Perplexed* III 16, 19–21; Thomas Aquinas, *Summa Theologica* Part I, Q. 14, Art. 8, 11, 13; Q. 57, Art. 2, 3) This argument could not have been known to Socrates or to Plato in the precise form that we know it. It may be useful, however, to consider *Lysis* 215a6–b2.

15. *Symposium* 202c6–d6.

(215a7–b3), neither would it love any other beings for whose sake it might pursue it. Thus, for example, it would not seek medical knowledge and would be forever ignorant of it.[16] More importantly, such a being would have no need to know what is good, in any given situation, for the whole human being. And since it would not need it, neither would it ever possess this wisdom, which we need if we are to be benefited by our possessions and to live happily or well (cf. 208e7–210c5).[17] If, then, wisdom includes practical knowledge, both of the arts and of the human good as a whole, an eternally self-sufficient being would never become wise.

We have seen that ignorance of human things would not be an evil for an eternally self-sufficient being. But it is frequently an evil for us, since we are subject to many other evils which compel us to act knowledgeably in order to escape them (cf. 209c2 and context).[18] We are often enough ill, for example, and aware of our illness, to recognize that some among us must know the medical art. Moreover, some human beings learn that they do not know who or what is good, that they do not know what way of life would be good for them or best for them. Such men recognize a need to know about these things, and who can set limits to how far their questioning might lead? Though we are not wise, we humans—and perhaps some other needy beings—are in a position to become in a sense wiser than the eternally self-sufficient. And though we are not ourselves good, we may also become in a sense better than such beings, for our wisdom would be a good for us, and to be good for human beings is one aspect of being good.[19] It

16. Cf. *Republic* 341e4–6.
17. Compare also *Euthydemus* 279d6–281e5; *Meno* 88a6–89a6.
18. Cf. *Statesman* 299e5–9.
19. Cf. *Republic* 505a2–b1.

may well be the case, then, that to be simply or unqualifiedly good is as impossible for the eternally self-sufficient as for us who are needy.

The argument that has just been outlined might also help to explain a curious lack of parallelism between Socrates' two examples. After stating that the body, because of the evil of disease, loves the medical art (217b3–4; 219a1–3), Socrates does not say that the soul, because of the evil of ignorance, loves wisdom. Instead, he speaks simply of the ones who possess ignorance in such a manner as to love wisdom, and he makes no mention of the soul or its loves. (Compare, however, 218b8 and 220c4.) But now, perhaps, we can make sense of this deviation from a strict analogy. What Socrates may mean is that the soul by itself, apart from the body, would not be a lover of wisdom in the full sense of the word. Just as the body would clearly be unable, in the absence of soul, to love the medical art, so also the presence of a body may be a condition for the love of wisdom. Although the soul may well be a learning soul, among other things, by nature, it would have no concern for knowledge of human things if it were unaffected by the body and its evils. And since human things are one part of the whole, a disembodied soul would not love knowledge as a whole. In this light, perhaps, we can also understand why Socrates in the *Phaedrus* fails to mention the good, and also courage, among the beings beheld by the deathless gods (*Phaedrus* 247c3–e6). It may require an acquaintance with evil, or a suffering being's concern for suffering beings, in order to know at least some aspects of what is good, just as courage in particular cannot be fully known by one who has never felt the mortal's fear of death. And here in the *Lysis,* Socrates seems to be suggesting that only composite, bodily beings such as ourselves possess that ignorance which, by appearing as an evil, leads to the love of wisdom as a whole. In other words, the evils associated with our perishable bodies are in a sense necessary evils, necessary in the sense that they could not be eliminated without the loss of philosophy and of wisdom.[20]

The significance, for the *Lysis* as a whole, of this extended discussion about philosophy and wisdom should become clearer by the end of the dialogue.

Socrates' Criticism of His Suggestion That the Friend Is a Friend of the Good (218c4–221d6)

SOCRATES' FEAR THAT HIS SUGGESTION MIGHT BE WRONG, AND HIS ELABORATION OF IT IN ORDER TO PREPARE FOR REFUTING IT (218c4–220b5)

Socrates relates to his present listener(s) that after the two boys agreed to his account of what the friend is, he himself rejoiced greatly. He was, as he says, like a hunter who had, to his satisfaction, what he had been hunting for himself. Though Socrates had been longing, ever since he was a boy, for the acquisition of friends, he was on this occasion content to seek knowledge of what a friend is. And he rejoiced to believe that he had found it. Socrates' joy, however, did not last long, for a most strange suspicion came over him that the things they had agreed to were untrue. Without a moment's hesitation, and without the slightest vanity, he tells the two

20. Cf. *Theaetetus* 176a5–b1.

boys of his doubts about what he had suggested. Lysis, who had eagerly agreed to what looked to be a firm conclusion, is silent now that it is questioned. Menexenus, however, asks Socrates what difficulty he sees. Socrates replies that he fears that their accounts about the friend have been false, in the way that boastful human beings are false.

The boastfulness of these accounts is, in part, simply their false claim to be true. But we may add, to anticipate what follows, that this latest argument still boasts, in the fashion of the poets,[21] by pretending that a friend is a higher being than he is. In particular, the friend has been said to be a friend of the good, which as such is also beautiful (216d2). As an example of such a good, Socrates has suggested wisdom, or being wise. And although our analysis has focused on that aspect of wisdom which is directed to action, there is also of course the theoretical aspect. Indeed, we tend to think of the highest wisdom—if not as a goddess (212d8) or a self-subsistent being —as a contemplative activity which is loved for its own sake more than for any useful consequences.[22] More broadly, we consider the good, as we do a true friend, to be lovable more for its own sake than for the benefit it brings us. And in so doing, we suppose ourselves to be "friends" who love the good for its own sake. This is in keeping with our assumption that the good is also beautiful or noble.[23] Socrates will confirm, in the ensuing discussion, that at least Menexenus thinks about the highest good in the manner just outlined. Yet precisely this thought, with its hidden assumption that we ourselves are "selfless" friends of the good, is a major element of the boastfulness which Socrates will now call into question.

21. Cf. pages 124–126 above; also 221d2–6.
22. Cf. *Republic* 357b4–d3, especially c1–3.
23. Cf. Aristotle *Rhetoric* 1366a33.

Socrates prepares the criticism of his suggestion about what a friend is with a more thorough and precise look into the question why a friend is a friend. He asks Menexenus whether whoever would be a friend is not also, in addition to being a friend to someone, a friend "for the sake of something" and "because of something." Or is he a friend "for the sake of nothing and because of nothing?" Menexenus replies that it is for the sake of something and because of something. Here we have the first thematic reference to that "for the sake of which" (*hou heneka*) a friend is a friend (cf. 215d6), or the end which the lover has in view. It is distinguished from that "because of which," that is, "as a result of which," (*dia ho*) a friend is a friend, or that evil whose presence compels him to pursue some good. And though Greek usage would not require this, each of the prepositional phrases is reserved in this passage for one of these two ways of answering the question "why?" The distinction is so strictly maintained that when Socrates once uses the preposition *heneka* with the apparent meaning "because of" (some evil), it will be jarring to the reader (220e4).[24] But that usage will be a deliberate anomaly, introduced in order to awaken an especially close attention to the difficult question of why the ultimate good is loved. For the immediate argument, however, it is easy enough to distinguish the evil because of which from the good for the sake of which the friend is a friend.

Socrates now asks whether that thing, for the sake of which the friend is a friend to its friend, is a friend or whether it is neither a friend nor an enemy. It is hardly surprising that Menexenus replies he cannot quite follow. Indeed, Socrates

---

24. This usage is anticipated at 219d7–e1. In connection with that passage, see note 70 to the accompanying translation.

even supposes that in trying to interpret what he means for Menexenus he will also understand it better himself (218e2–3; cf. 216c4–5). The full understanding of his own insights requires that they be articulated in speech, and perhaps also illustrated by example. At any rate, Socrates now returns to the use of examples, and from this concession to Menexenus he also expects to win further clarity for himself. The fact that even an alert "follower" of his argument can be of use to Socrates in his philosophizing is not a negligible factor in explaining his fondness for conversation with the young.[25]

The example to which Socrates turns is the now familiar one of the patient's love for the doctor. Yet in the light of Socrates' recent discussion of philosophy, the reader should also keep in mind that he has told Lysis earlier that everyone would love him if he were to become wise (210d1–2). Both doctors and the wise are loved as knowers (cf. 215d5–7). To begin his elucidation, Socrates reminds Menexenus that they had spoken of the one who is ill as a friend of the doctor. Next, he asks whether the patient is not a friend of the doctor because of disease and for the sake of health. Menexenus agrees that this is so. What has emerged, in other words, is that the

25. "Certain it is that whosoever hath his mind fraught with many thoughts, his wits and understanding do clarify and break up, in the communicating and discoursing with another; he tosseth his thoughts more easily; he marshalleth them more orderly; he seeth how they look when they are turned into words; finally, he waxeth wiser than himself, and that more by an hour's discourse than by a day's meditation. . . . Neither is this second fruit of friendship, in opening the understanding, restrained only to such friends as are able to give a man counsel; (they indeed are best;) but even without that, a man learneth of himself, and bringeth his own thoughts to light, and whetteth his wits as against a stone, which itself cuts not." Francis Bacon, "Of Friendship," *Essays or Counsels Civil and Moral.* Compare *Parmenides* 137b6–8.

doctor is not loved for his own sake by the patient, but rather for the sake of (the patient's) health. In answer to Socrates' further questions, Menexenus gives the obvious replies that disease is an evil and health a good. What they were saying, then, continues Socrates, seems to be that the body, which is neither good nor bad, is a friend of the medical art, which is a good, because of the evil of disease. And he adds that the medical art has accepted the friendship for the sake of health, which is a good. Menexenus agrees that this is what they were saying.

Menexenus fails to observe, however, that Socrates did not make the expected remark that the body is a friend of the medical art, which is a good, for the sake of the further good of health. Instead, he spoke of the medical art as having accepted the friendship with the body for the sake of health— that is to say, for the sake of the body's health. The medical art, which is itself a good, is naturally directed to securing the good of something else.[26] And even if this is not a "love" of the body, it is hard to account for in terms of Socrates' suggestion that the friend is not good, but a sufferer from the presence of evil. Socrates' use of the word "friendship," moreover, reminds us of another limitation of the present discussion. It reminds us of the reciprocity implied in friendship, a reciprocity which Socrates has ignored since offering his own suggestion about the friend (cf. 216c1–3). Indeed, Socrates will follow up this hint later in the dialogue and rectify his failure to account for reciprocal friendship here. But for now, his brief reminder of reciprocal friendship, and of a love for the good of another, calls our attention to the absence of these considerations in the passage immediately to follow.

26. Cf. *Republic* 341d7–342c2.

Socrates continues his argument as if he had spoken, not of the medical art, but merely of the body as a friend of health. He leads Menexenus to affirm that health is a friend (or something dear) and disease an enemy. It follows, then, according to Socrates, that what is neither good nor bad is a friend of the good because of what is bad and an enemy, and for the sake of what is good and a friend. Menexenus replies that it appears so. Socrates then refines this conclusion into the statement that what is a friend is a friend (or dear) for the sake of the friend (that is, of what is dear) and because of the enemy. "It seems so," says Menexenus.

Socrates now tells the two boys that since they have arrived at this point, they should pay close attention lest they be deceived. He will stress his concern with the danger of deception by mentioning it twice again in the immediate sequel (219b6; cf. 219b9; d2–4). Although the risk of being deceived exists in any discussion, it is of particular importance in the inquiry concerning what a friend is. For if what we say about friends deceives us, and especially if it deceives us into thinking that they are more than they are in fact (cf. 218d2–4), our mistaken speech could well lead us to think we have been deceived by our friends themselves. In continuing his argument, Socrates says next that he will let it pass that what is a friend has become a friend of the friend or, in other words, that what is like becomes a friend of its like—which they had declared to be impossible. Apparently, he means by this that he intends to ignore the specious objection that since likes cannot be friends, then a friend cannot be a friend to its friend. But by explicitly dismissing the statement that the friend has become a friend of the friend, Socrates calls attention more importantly to the fact that he had not quite said this in his most recent conclusion. He had, indeed, suggested it a little earlier (218d9–10), but the conclusion was merely that the friend is a friend for the sake of the friend—not that it is a friend of the friend. (Concerning the text here, see note 67 of the translation.) Moreover, the argument which is to come suggests that the absence of this latter phrase was intentional, for the argument will show that in an important respect the friend is not a friend of his friend. In fact, it is largely in order to prepare for this surprising consequence that Socrates speaks so emphatically here of the danger of deception.

Socrates now suggests that they consider the following matter so as not to be deceived by what is being said. He reminds Menexenus that the medical art, as they assert, is a friend (that is, dear) for the sake of health. Menexenus agrees to this restatement, but in so doing he fails to notice a change which Socrates has introduced in his use of the word "friend." Instead of speaking, as he had done, of the intermediate lover as the friend of the good, Socrates here begins to apply the word "friend" to that good which is loved (219c2; cf. 216c3; 216e7–217a2; 218b8–c2).[27] The new usage, however, makes sense when we consider that a man who loves someone else tends to forget himself, and his deficiencies, and to dwell instead upon the perfections of his friend. Similarly, the lover of some excellence (for example, wisdom) characteristically directs his thought away from himself and toward that good for which he strives. By applying the word friend (or dear) to the good which is loved, rather than to the lover himself, Socrates imitates this self-forgetfulness and prepares his ripening criticism of their "boastful" speeches about the friend.

Socrates continues by saying that if health is a friend (or

27. This change had been anticipated at 218d10 and 219b6–7. See also 216c6–7.

dear), then it too is a friend for the sake of something. Moreover, it follows from their argument that that for whose sake health is a friend is also a friend itself. This reasoning, as Menexenus sees, threatens to go on indefinitely. Yet if every friend were a friend for the sake of another friend, then their account of what a friend is would always presuppose that which they are trying to account for. They would always, in other words, be infinitely far from understanding what a friend is, or what is dear. Therefore, Socrates tells Menexenus that they must necessarily either abandon this way of proceeding or else arrive at some first principle. Such a first principle, he continues, would no longer bring them back to another friend, but would have come to (or "would be related to") that which is a friend in the first place, that for the sake of which they say that the other things are also all friends. (It is not wholly clear from this statement whether the first principle is itself the friend in the first place, or whether it is somehow immediately related to it. Yet in the immediate sequel, Socrates will ignore any possible distinction between the first principle and the primary friend.) Menexenus agrees that these are necessarily their only alternatives.

In continuing his argument, Socrates silently disregards the possibility that all friends, or dear things, might be loved for the sake of still further friends. Indeed, the dismissal of this alternative is so unobtrusive that Menexenus seems not even to notice it. Yet even though Socrates gives no reason for excluding this possibility, his choice to do so makes sense. For it is not merely the present course of inquiry which requires the supposition of a "first friend" if it is to go on. To see this, let us recall that a friend, in this context, is said to be someone like the doctor, who is loved because he is good, that is, good for the sake of something else. Now an analogous account can be presented which extends well beyond what we usually think of as friendly love. In fact, it can be applied to the great majority of our serious pursuits, in which we seek to obtain or to accomplish what we regard as good, that is, good for the sake of something further. Yet in all these cases it would be absurd for us to say that we seek, or love, such goods as goods if there were nothing which we loved in itself and for whose sake we pursued the merely instrumental goods. In other words, Socrates' original suggestion about the friend, along with all that we say when we strive for some good, presupposes that there is (at least) one first or ultimate "friend." And only by accepting this presupposition can Socrates bring to light the full implications of his suggestion about the friend and of our serious speech about the good. Accordingly, then, he continues the discussion as if this presupposition were established.

Now that he has introduced the boys to the "first friend," or the "primary dear thing," Socrates finally explains why he had warned against their being deceived by what was being said. He tells them of his suspicion that all other things which they call friends for the sake of that one are like deceptive phantoms of it, while the first one is that which is in truth a friend. In other words, the phantom friends may deceive us into believing that they are truly friends. To illustrate how he means this, Socrates turns to a new example. And though the example speaks of those we make much of, and not directly of friends, it is still relevant, for Socrates had already argued that only those who make much of one another can be one another's friends (215b7–c2ff). Sometimes, says Socrates, a father values his son more highly than all his other possessions. (Even the son, by this account, is a possession, albeit a highly valued one.) Will not such a father, Socrates asks, also make much of something else on account of his considering his son worth everything (*heneka tou . . . hēgeisthai,* 219d7–e1)?[28] If, for example, he should notice that his son had drunk hemlock, would he not also make much of wine if he thought that it could save his son? "Of course," replies Menexenus, and reasonably so. We know that a father in these circumstances would be willing to give up a great deal for this antidote. Socrates then extends his reasoning to the vessel which holds the wine. Does this mean, Socrates now asks, that the father would at that time make no more of his own son than of an earthenware cup, and no more than of a pint and a half of wine? Or is it rather that all such seriousness is not directed to those things which are provided for the sake of something, but to that, the son, for the sake of which all such things are provided? Socrates acknowledges that we often say that we make much of gold and silver. But he adds that this is still not the truth. Rather, he says, what we regard as everything is that—whatever it comes to light as being—for the sake of which gold and silver and all provisions are provided. Menexenus agrees that this is so. Returning now to his account of the friend, Socrates contends that all those things which they call friends (or dear) for the sake of some other friend are manifestly friends in name only. It may be, he concludes, that what is really a friend, or dear, is that itself into which all these so-called friendships (*hautai hai legomenai philiai,* 220b2–3) terminate. Menexenus agrees that this may be so, and Socrates adds that what is really a friend, or dear, is not a friend for the sake of some friend.

We of course want to know how Socrates understands the true friend. But first we must ask about those "phantoms" of

28. See note 70 to the accompanying translation.

it which deceive us into regarding them as friends although they are so in name only. What are these "phantoms"? The conclusion which suggests itself is that they include all those human beings whom we ordinarily call our "friends." This becomes clear if we return to Socrates' original suggestion about the friend. Had he said merely that whatever is good is loved, then all those who are good could be loved as friends. But his account also required that the lover himself must suffer from the presence of evils if he is to love the good (218b8–c3). In other words, we do not love anyone as a friend, in the fullest sense, unless we also make much of him, and we do not (wisely) make much of those whom we do not need for ourselves (215b3–c2). Someone who is healthy, for example, would not love a doctor, as doctor, no matter how good he might be at his art (217a6). Another way of presenting this argument is to say that we love others as friends, not simply because they are good, but rather for the sake of that good which they provide for us. Yet to the extent that this is so, we do not truly love these "friends" at all. What we love instead, and what might truly be dear or a friend, is that further good which we need and which we use them for. According to this understanding, for example, not even the man who is ill truly loves the doctor as a friend, since his need of him is for the sake of his health. Yet this conclusion, however harsh it seems, is not wholly strange. In our ordinary understanding we distinguish true friends from those we "love," or use, for the sake of some advantage (220b4–7; cf. 207c10–11).[29] What Socrates has done is to combine this awareness with his own suggestion that no one loves another as a friend, in the fullest sense, unless he needs him and finds him useful. From this

---

29. Cf. Aristotle, *Nicomachean Ethics* 1156a10–12; 1157a14–16.

combination it follows that no human being, nor any other living being, however good, is truly or fully a friend to another.

Socrates' suspicions about what is truly a friend, and its deceptive phantoms, have particular significance in relation to his earlier conversation with Lysis. There he had argued that if Lysis were to become wise, then everyone would love him as a friend, since he would be useful and good (210c7–d4). We have already suggested some possible weaknesses in this argument. But the most serious among them emerges here. For if Lysis, or anyone else, were to become wise, all those who would "love" him for his wisdom would not truly love him at all. Those who might be content to be ruled by his wisdom would not be lovers of Lysis, but rather of the good of being well governed. And those not content to be ruled by another, and who would seek from him instead the wisdom to guide themselves, might conceivably become lovers of wisdom, but they would not become lovers of Lysis. Lysis could never become wise, or even aware of his own ignorance, unless he were first to free himself from the belief that as a wise man he could fully satisfy his desire to be loved. In keeping with this we note that though Socrates has spoken loosely of the patient as a friend of the doctor (217a6–7; 218e3–5), he does not similarly misrepresent the lovers of wisdom as lovers of the wise (218a2–b3).[30] Though lovers of wisdom might seek out those already wise—if there are any—in order to learn from them, they would not be deceived into regarding them as friends in the fullest sense.

30. Contrast the language of Socrates' anonymous interlocutor at 215d4–7.

SOCRATES' PRIMARY REFUTATION
(220b6–220e6)

By distinguishing what is really a friend from those "friends" that are loved for its sake, Socrates has clarified the meaning of his original suggestion that friendly love is of the good. But he has not yet shown why he feared that the suggestion was false (218c7–d4), and consequently he now turns to this task. He reminds Menexenus that they have dismissed the notion that the friend is a friend for the sake of some friend. "But then is the good a friend?" he asks. Menexenus sees no reason to retreat from this aspect of Socrates' account,[31] and he replies that this is his opinion. From this response we learn that Menexenus is convinced that there is some ultimate good, whether simple or composite, loved for its own sake and not for the sake of some further dear thing. We might also surmise that he regards this good—which is also beautiful, in his opinion (216d2–3)—as a common good, a good that can be shared. Wisdom, for example, might well appear as something that can be shared and as at least an element of the ultimate good. Accordingly, Menexenus may suppose that human beings, whether or not they can be true friends of each other, can be united in a common pursuit.[32] This, however, is merely a surmise. What is clear is Menexenus' conviction that the good, whatever it may be, is loved for itself or for its own sake. Yet Socrates proceeds to call into question precisely this conviction. And by so doing he also

31. See page 165 above.
32. Consider the plural *hēmin* at 220a7 and compare *Symposium* 205a5–8.

compels us to wonder whether even the good itself is truly dear, or a friend.

In order to show the weakness of the position they have reached, Socrates asks what would happen to our love of the good if there were no longer any evil. To begin with, he recalls their agreement that the good is loved because of what is bad. He then asks Menexenus to pretend that the bad were to depart, and that only what is good and what is neither good nor bad were left remaining. And if what is bad, he continues, were to lay hold of neither any body, nor any soul, nor any of the other things which are themselves in themselves neither bad nor good, would the good be in no way useful to us, and would it have become useless? Menexenus has no answer to this question, so Socrates proceeds to explain why it would make sense to say yes. If nothing, he says, were to harm us any longer, we would require no benefit, and thus it would become manifest then that we had been treasuring and loving the good because of what is bad, as if the good were a drug against what is bad, and the bad a disease. And if there is no disease, he goes on, then a drug is not required. Socrates is suggesting, in other words, that if there were no longer any evil (that is, anything bad) the good would no longer be needed, and so would no longer be loved. But if this is so, we must reconsider also the character of our present love of the good. Accordingly, Socrates asks if the good is of such a nature as to be loved by us—who are in the middle of the bad and the good—because of what is bad, while it is of no use itself for its own sake. Menexenus replies that this seems to be so. What Socrates means here is that the very nature of the good, insofar as it is good (as distinct from beautiful), is to be good for someone. But the good could not be good for anyone if there were no one who needed it, and no one would need it were it not for the presence, or threatened presence, of evils. No matter, then, how one conceives of the good—whether as wisdom, or as wisdom together with pleasure,[33] or as virtue, or as virtue together with happiness, or whatever—it is not good for its own sake. It is good for beings like us, and as a remedy against the evils from which we suffer. If, then, there were no evil, "the good" would be good for no one, and as a consequence it would not *be* at all, any more than there are trees which are not trees.[34]

Having argued this much about the nature of the good, Socrates now suggests why the good might not be truly a friend. He does this by contrasting the ultimate good with those other goods, or good beings, that we love. That friend of ours, he says, into which all the others were seen to terminate and for whose sake they were called "friends," has no resemblance to them. For they, he continues, were called friends for the sake of a friend, while what is really a friend, or dear, comes to light as being of a nature wholly the opposite. "For it has appeared plainly to be a friend to us for the sake of an enemy (*echthrou heneka*, 220e4); and if what is an enemy [or hated] would go away, it is no longer, as it seems, a friend to us." This conclusion would be hardly more than a restatement were it not for the strange phrase "for the sake of an enemy," where we would have expected "because of an enemy" (*dia echthron*). But as it is, we are astonished by the thought that the ultimate good might be loved *for the sake of* (*heneka*) an enemy, or something hated. Scholars have attempted various explanations of this oddity. Hans von Arnim, for example, thought that Plato deliberately employed a logical blunder in

33. Cf. *Republic* 505b5–c5.
34. Cf. *Theaetetus* 176a5, and see Xenophon, *Memorabilia* III viii 2–3.

order to ridicule the entire notion that the Good is loved even because of evil, let alone for the sake of it, or for any other reason outside of itself.[35] Paul Shorey, on the other hand considered that the preposition *heneka* no longer means "for the sake of," but merely "because of." He explains this unusual—for the *Lysis*—usage as Plato's way of making the antithesis between that which is truly a friend and the other "friends" "as complete, as emphatic, and as symmetrical as possible."[36] It seems, however, that *heneka* must be translated in its strong sense, for only by claiming that the good is loved "for the sake of an enemy" (*echthrou heneka*) can Socrates present it as entirely opposite (*pan tounantion,* 220e3) to the other friends, which are loved "for the sake of a friend" (*philou heneka,* 220e2). And more importantly, this more extreme interpretation offers an insight into the truest reason for Socrates' doubts that friendly love is of the good (cf. 218c5–d4). For if the good is loved for the sake of something else, then according to the argument it is that something else—and not the good—which is really the friend (cf. 219c2–d2 and 219e7–220a1).

But what could that be for whose sake the ultimate good is loved? The only answer that makes sense is that it is, for each of us, himself. We have already seen that we do not love the good for its own sake, but because we need it ourselves. This is to say, however, that each of us loves what is good for his own sake. But from this it follows that each of us, to the extent that his love is love of the good, is his own true or primary friend (cf. 219c2–4). And this is the case no matter

35. *Platos Jugenddialoge und die Entstehungszeit des Phaidros* (Leipzig, 1914), pp. 54–55.

36. "The Alleged Fallacy in Plato *Lysis* 220e," *Classical Philology* 25 (1930), 382.

how "common" the good might be. Indeed, there is evidence
in support of this interpretation even in the very passage
where Plato's Diotima appears to be asserting its opposite
(*Symposium* 205e1–206a1; cf. 204e2–4). To illustrate her claim
that men love nothing but what is good, she refers to those
who are willing to have their own limbs amputated if those
limbs should seem bad to them. But if we ask why men are
willing to undergo amputation, we see that they do so in
order to preserve their lives—in other words, for the sake of
themselves. More broadly stated, the source of men's rejection
of what belongs to them most intimately, and of their willingness to suffer in pursuit of the good, is their love of
themselves.[37]

The above suggestion, however, though it may explain
how the good is loved for the sake of something else, does not
yet account for Socrates' speaking of the ultimate friend as a
friend "for the sake of *an enemy.*" Yet even this makes sense if
we recall that those who "love" the good do so because of the
presence of some evil. For even though we who love the good
because of the presence of evil are not yet bad ourselves, we
would not love it unless we hated our present bad (for example, ignorant) condition. One can therefore say—speaking
loosely—that we hate ourselves, or that the being for whose
sake we love the good is an enemy. Upon a closer look, however, it becomes clear that we would not hate our present bad
condition, and seek to improve it, if we did not in a truer
sense love ourselves (cf. 207d5–7). It is because we love ourselves that we also "love" the good, for the good is a remedy
against the evils which hinder or threaten to hinder us from

37. For the distinction between "oneself" and "what belongs to
oneself," see *Alcibiades I* 127e9–128d10ff.

being ourselves—whatever being ourselves might turn out to be. Or, since we cannot, and should not, love even ourselves unreservedly so long as our life is obstructed by the presence of evils,[38] it is better to say not that we love ourselves, but that we love for ourselves to be ourselves, that is, to be free of serious evils. And were we free of evils, we would then love for ourselves to continue to be in that condition.

On the basis of this strict interpretation of Socrates' argument, even the ultimate good is another "phantom" of the real friend. The real friend, for each of us, is "himself," or himself as he would be if he were free of evils. It may be true, then, as Socrates says, that the good would no longer be a friend to us if "the enemy" were to go away (once and for all). Yet the real friend might still remain, since each of us— who himself in himself (220c4–5), is neither bad nor good— might still remain as a friend to himself. Each of us would love himself then, as he loves himself now, not because he was good but simply because it is his nature to do so—his nature, at least, once he becomes aware of himself in his distinctness from all others.[39]

SOCRATES' REFUTATION AS PRESENTED FOR MENEXENUS (220e6–221d6)

Despite the importance of the conclusion that Socrates has reached, Menexenus seems to understand it only in its weaker sense. Apparently, he does not interpret Socrates to be saying

38. Cf. *Gorgias* 512a2–b2.
39. Concerning the posibility of this kind of self-awareness, see C. Bruell, "Socratic Politics and Self-Knowledge," pp. 171–172, 175–176.

that the good is itself loved "for the sake of" something else, but rather "because of" something else. What he assents to—hesitantly—is merely the proposition that the good would no longer be a friend to us if what is bad were out of the way. Socrates, however, does not repeat himself or otherwise attempt to share his most radical thought with the boy. Rather than try to impose upon him the sobriety of his own understanding, he modifies his refutation of the claim that love is of the good. And he will punctuate this modified conclusion explicitly enough for Menexenus to follow it.

To begin the new stage of his argument, Socrates asks, with an oath by Zeus, whether there will no longer be hungering, thirsting, or the like if what is bad ceases to be. Or will there, he continues, still be hunger, if indeed there are humans and the other living beings, but without its being harmful? And will there also be thirst, he asks, and the other desires, but without their being bad, inasmuch as what is bad will have ceased to be? What Socrates is asking, in other words, is whether to be without evils means also to be without desires, and without the temporary pains (and pleasures) associated with the desires. It seems that it might not, at least not if humans and the other living beings would still remain in the absence of evils, for what is to be alive, if not to desire? But is the life of human beings possible, as distinct from being merely imaginable, in the absence of such serious evils as death? Instead of dwelling, however, upon questions like these, Socrates wonders whether it isn't ludicrous to ask what will be or will not be then, that is, when there are no longer any evils. "For who knows?" By this question Socrates calls attention to the poverty of our experience in this whole sphere. He thus interrupts any dreams we might be entertaining and provides a timely reminder of how small a share we humans have of that good, whatever it might be, which could serve us as a drug against evils.

To return the conversation to the sphere of our experience, Socrates observes that we do know it is possible even for one who is hungry to be harmed, as well as to be benefited. We know, in other words, that a hungry man might improve or harm his health by eating, just as he might do either by not eating, depending upon the circumstances.[40] Socrates continues by asking whether it is also possible for one who is thirsty, or who has all the other such desires, sometimes to desire beneficially, sometimes harmfully, and sometimes neither. As for those desires which are neither beneficial nor harmful, Socrates is probably thinking of those which—though they may be painful in themselves or pleasant in their being satisfied—are neither helpful nor harmful to the health of one's body or the condition of one's soul. Menexenus replies with unusual vehemence that the outcomes which Socrates has mentioned are all possible. If, then, asks Socrates, evils are ceasing to be, what connection do they have with the things which do not happen to be evils, so that these should be ceasing to be along with the evils? When Menexenus answers that there is no such connection, Socrates concludes that there will still be those desires which are neither good nor bad even if there cease to be any evils. To this conclusion Menexenus responds cautiously that it appears so. We should observe here that Socrates does not say that the good or beneficial desires would also remain if there were no longer any evils. Yet his silence about such desires makes sense by now, for there is indeed a connection between good desires and the presence of evils. In the absence of evils, there would no longer be any

40. Cf. *Gorgias* 499c6–e3.

need of or any use for good things, at least not insofar as they were good. And as a result, good desires, insofar as they were good, would no longer remain. There might still, of course, be those desires, such as thirst, or the thirst for knowledge, which can be good for us now; but though they could still bring pleasure, they would no longer be needed or good.

Now that he has secured Menexenus' agreement that some desires would remain even if evils ceased to be, Socrates proceeds to challenge openly his original suggestion about the friend. He asks Menexenus whether it is possible for one who desires and loves passionately (*epithymounta te kai erōnta,* 221b7) not to love as a friend (*philein,* 221b8) that which he desires and loves passionately. Menexenus replies that this is impossible, at least in his opinion. Apparently, then, continues Socrates, there will still be some things which are friends (*phil'atta,* 221c1), even if evils cease to be. Yet if what is bad, he says, were a cause of a thing's being a friend, and it ceased to be, nothing would then be a friend to another. For if a cause ceased to be, he continues, it would presumably be impossible for there still to be that thing which had this cause. Menexenus replies that this is correct. Now then, resumes Socrates, they have agreed that the friend loves (*philein,* 221c6) something and because of something. And previously, he adds, they supposed that whatever is neither good nor bad loves what is good because of what is bad. But now, he says, there appears some other cause of loving and being loved (*tou philein te kai phileisthai,* 221d2). "It seems so," says Menexenus. Socrates concludes by asking whether desire is really a cause of friendship and whether what desires is a friend to that which it desires and at the time when it desires. "And as for what we were previously saying to be a friend, was it some kind of idle talk, like a long poem strung together?" "I'm afraid so," replies Menexenus.

This argument serves to remind us of a most important aspect of friendship, one which Socrates' earlier suggestion had neglected. For we humans, as social animals, naturally desire to be together with one another, and from the time that we are children we long to be with friends. The immediacy of this desire, like that of the desire for food or drink, shows it to be independent of our concern with, and thought about, the good (cf. 211d7–8). Moreover, we know from experience that those whose company we most enjoy are not always the ones who are best or whom we most need to have as friends. In keeping with this, and by noting that friendly desire could still remain in the absence of evils, Socrates appears to refute his earlier assertion that what is bad is responsible for something being a friend (that is, a friend of the good). And he appears to establish instead that desire is the cause of friendship. This, at any rate, is the conclusion to which he leads Menexenus.

If we look more closely, however, we see that Socrates' claim is probably the more limited one that desire is *a* cause of friendship. And indeed his restraint on this point is reasonable, for his argument has left open the possibility that what is bad, while not being the sole cause, might still be *a* cause of something being a friend. And if what is bad were one of several causes, there might still be friendship in the absence of evils. Its character, however, would be different from that of friendship as we know it now. From here the suggestion emerges that two causes must be present for there to be friends in the fullest sense of the word. That is to say, there must be on the one hand evils—and the desire for good which arises once they are recognized as such (cf. 217b7–c1; e6–9)—and on the other hand those more immediate desires which arise without prior reflection. Someone who is ill, for example, no matter how much he needed his doctor, would not truly love him as a friend unless he would desire his company in health as well as in sickness. And equally, childhood playmates would not yet be true friends, however much they desired to be together. Without the experience of those serious concerns in which one needs a friend, they would not treasure each other, or wish to treasure each other, in a fully human way (cf. 214e5–215a3). Instead of refuting Socrates' original suggestion, then, this new one could appear as a complement to it. Indeed, the inadequacy of this manifest refutation helps to confirm the significance of the earlier, or "hidden," one. But if we ignore for now the question of self-love, as well as the deceptiveness of what were called "phantoms" of the good, the difficulty of friendship can be stated as follows. Friendship in the fullest sense is a hybrid, and it requires the coincidence of two causes—affectionate desire and a need for the good— that have no necessary connection with one another.

The Kindred as Friends
(221d6–222d8)

Socrates' Alternative Suggestion That Friendship Is Love of the Kindred for the Kindred

For the time being, at any rate, Socrates continues with the argument as if it had been agreed that desire is the sole cause of friendship (see, however, 222b7–c1). In order to examine further the character of such friendship, he considers the question of what desire is for. That which desires, he suggests, desires whatever it is in want of, or whatever it lacks. When Menexenus agrees that this is so, Socrates then asks whether what is in want is a friend of that which it is in want of. (He does not assert this as his own opinion.) Menexenus replies that this is his opinion, and Socrates continues by asserting that something becomes in want of whatever it is deprived of. From all this Socrates concludes, tentatively, that passionate love (*erōs*), friendship, and desire happen to be for what is akin, or for what is one's own (*tou oikeiou dē, hōs eoiken*, 221e3). In drawing this conclusion, he addresses both of the boys by name, and for the first time in quite a while Lysis joins Menexenus in assenting to what Socrates has said (cf. 218c2–3). Taking advantage of his opportunity to converse with the two of them together, Socrates tells them that if they are friends to each other (*allēlois*, 221e6) they are by nature in some way akin to each other (*hymin autois*).

A hint as to how Socrates understands the love of what is akin is his use as synonyms, in this last sentence, of the reciprocal and reflexive pronouns. That is to say, he uses a word for "each other" which can also mean "yourselves".[1] In this way Socrates suggests that the very distinction between self and other becomes blurred in this friendship, or that the two friends become in a sense one.[2] Now that desire, in other words, is thought of as love of the kindred, it is no longer merely a desire for the pleasures of companionship. It is no longer, in fact, like any desire, or need, to acquire what belongs naturally to a single human being; instead, the desire or longing of each being is to belong to a larger whole of which he is merely a part. (Contrast with this Socrates' statement of his own desire for the acquisition or possession of friends, at 211d7–e8 ff.) Such erotic longing is a sign that we humans are partial beings, who become whole, as it seems, by surrendering ourselves to that larger whole to which we naturally belong. The love of one's kindred, then, or of one's own, is ultimately a love for union with one's own.[3] Yet the kindred friends never become so united as to lose completely

1. Cf. *Phaedrus* 255d6, and notes 52 and 82 to the accompanying translation.

2. Compare Aristophanes' speech in the *Symposium,* especially 191d1–2 and 192d2–e9.

3. "*Liebe heisst überhaupt das Bewusstsein meiner Einheit mit einem Anderen, so dass ich für mich nicht isoliert bin, sondern mein Selbstbewusstsein nur als Aufgebung meines Fürsichseins gewinne, und durch das mich wissen, als der Einheit meiner mit der Anderen, und des Anderen mit mir. . . .*" Hegel, *Grundlinien der Philosophie des Rechts,* Paragraph 158, Addition. [Love is, in general, the consciousness of my union with another, so that I am not self-centered and isolated, but gain my self-consciousness only as a giving up of my being self-centered and thereby know myself as the union of myself with the other and of the other with me.]

the distinctness which allows them to love each other as other. Despite the tendency to identify oneself with the other, and to love the whole which they comprise, the love of one's kindred remains also, somehow, the love of one being for another (*ei ara tis heteros heterou epithymei,* 221e7; cf. 221c3 and 212a6). In fact, this aspect of the love of one's kindred distinguishes it sharply from the love of the good, since the latter has come to light, not as love for another, but as the love of using others for the benefit of oneself.

In addition to calling the two boys akin to each other, Socrates speaks of them as akin "in some way by nature" (*physei pēi,* 221e6). And his following remark spells out in more detail what he means by a kinship "by nature." If someone desires another, he says, or loves him passionately, he would never desire, nor love passionately, nor love as a friend unless he happened to be akin in some way to his beloved—either in his soul, or else in some character of his soul, or some of its ways or some aspect of it. Now by interpreting natural kinship as a kinship of the soul, Socrates is making an important, if implicit, denial. His silence about the most usual kinship, which is the kinship within a family, implies that familial kinship is not truly by nature. We have suggested earlier that love within the family, and especially parental love, could not be sufficiently accounted for merely in terms of love of the good.[4] It is understood much more simply as a love of one's own, or a love of the kindred. Yet in the present account, one's relatives are supplanted as the truly natural kin by those with kindred souls (cf. 210c1–3). The kinship of relatives, in other words, even of those who love each other and do not just treat each other as possessions, or as "the necessary ones" (*hoi*

4. Cf. pp. 100–101 above. See also 212e7–213a3 and 219d5–e2.

anankaioi),[5] is not natural in the strict sense. For the family does not maintain itself by nature alone, but is supported by convention or by the laws (cf. 223a–b).[6] And since family kinship is not so truly natural, even a loving parent does not, as parent, love so genuinely as a true lover does.[7] This is not to deny that sometimes, or perhaps frequently, there might also be a natural kinship of soul between members of the same family. Yet this latter kinship remains the heart of all genuine friendship of one for another.

Menexenus readily assents to Socrates' statement that whoever loves another must be somehow akin to him in his soul. Lysis, however, remains silent. Though this is not the first time that Lysis silently drops out of the converstion (cf. 216a3; 218d1), it is the only occasion where Socrates' narration explicitly calls our attention to his silence. Apparently, then, this is a more significant silence than the earlier ones. Socrates continues by saying that "it has come to light as necessary for us to love (*philein*) what is akin by nature." Menexenus agrees that this seems so, but Lysis maintains his silence. We suspect that he had already anticipated this consequence of Socrates' argument and had become silently thoughtful about his own relation to his lover Hippothales.

Socrates now draws the decisive conclusion that it is necessary for the genuine, and not pretended, lover (*erastēi*, 222a7) to be loved (*phileisthai*) by his favorite (or favorites). If someone genuinely loves another, and not merely his own pleasure or advantage from the other, his love is necessarily requited. This conclusion, which may seem paradoxical, is less

5. Cf. *Republic* 574b12–c5.
6. See also *Crito* 50d2–5 and *Protagoras* 337c7–d3.
7. Cf. *Phaedrus* 255b3–7.

so once we recall that the return of love is not necessarily the return of sexual desire, and that it does not prevent the beloved from loving others as well. (Consider the change from the dual to the plural number in the verbs at 221e6.) Socrates' conclusion, moreover, follows directly from the understanding of love as love of one's kindred, since kinship, as distinct from mere ownership, is by its nature reciprocal. One cannot be akin to another without the other being akin to oneself. Accordingly, a genuine love of one's natural kin is of necessity returned.[8]

Neither Lysis nor Menexenus says anything in response to Socrates' conclusion, but they both, with difficulty, somehow nod their assent. We cannot be sure what they are thinking, but as regards Lysis, his lover Hippothales believes—and probably rightly—that he is at last confessing to love him in return. Hippothales' state of mind is evident from Socrates' description of him, for he is seen to radiate all sorts of colors as a result of his pleasure. He delights in the belief that he is loved by his beloved. As for Menexenus, he is perhaps reflecting that he will probably no longer remain Lysis' most intimate companion if Lysis should admit to Hippothales that he loves him. Or perhaps also Menexenus' silence stems from bashfulness at becoming aware that he too loves someone whom he regards as a "genuine lover." That is to say, he may already be aware of the love which will lead him, later, to become among the most devoted companions of Socrates.[9] But this is only conjecture. Clearly, however, Hippothales must now consider that

8. Cf. *Phaedrus* 255a1–c2; See also Goethe, *Elective Affinities,* Part II, chapter 7: *"Jede Anziehung ist wechselseitig."* "Every attraction is reciprocal."

9. See the *Menexenus* as a whole, and in particular 234b3–4. See, above all, *Phaedo* 59b9.

his appeal to Socrates for help in courting Lysis has been a great success. And it is almost equally clear that this moment marks a rupture in the friendship of Menexenus and Lysis.

Socrates, however, unlike his young companions, does not seem to be so moved at the conclusion of this argument as he was when it appeared that the friend was a friend of the good (cf. 218c4–5). He indicates the reason for his reserve as he proceeds to examine the argument. If what is akin, he says, differs in some respect from the like, then they might be saying something concerning what a friend is. But if, he adds, it happens that like and akin are the same, then it is not easy to reject the previous argument that what is like is useless to its like insofar as there is likeness (cf. 214e3–215a4). "And it is out of tune to agree that what is useless is a friend."

Socrates can argue in this fashion because he resists the charms of acknowledged reciprocal friendship. One of those charms, as has already been suggested, is the friends' illusion that they are self-sufficiently good and thus free of any need for what is useful. This may be called the charm of being loved. Yet there is also the still deeper charm of (requited) loving. Friends and lovers may well know that they are indeed deficient when apart, but they regard themselves as being free of evils so long as they remain together. Each tends to believe that their union itself is enough to satisfy his deepest longing, a longing not merely to acquire something useful for himself, but rather to become fully himself as a part of a larger whole. And the friends hope that this union in which they feel so at home will be everlasting. Socrates, however, implies that the union which they desire is unattainable for human beings, since our bodies—if nothing else—are naturally and unavoidably private.[10] He may also suspect, moreover, that even if

10. Cf. *Laws* 739c2–d3ff.

some god were to grant to friends a complete and never-ending union,[11] they would not yet be self-sufficient or free of evils. To judge from Aristophanes' speech in the *Symposium*, at any rate, our "ancestors," who were whole in the way that we long to become whole, were nevertheless unable to live contentedly or well (*Symposium* 190b5–d1; 193a1–3). As a result of considerations like these, then, Socrates does not allow the charming illusion of friendly union to obscure the fact that each of us, alone and by himself, suffers from evils and must love what is useful. Therefore, he concludes that the kindred could not be a friend—that is, a friend in the fullest sense—if it is not somehow useful to its friend.

The awareness of ourselves as separate, and in need of the useful, destroys the illusion that we might become contented and forever whole by surrendering ourselves wholly to friend-ship. Yet this awareness is still compatible with a desire, if somewhat attenuated, to be together with our natural kin, simply because they are akin to us. Moreover, as Socrates has argued earlier, we would not treasure our friends as we do unless we supposed, among other things, that we needed them for ourselves. It might appear, then, that this latest con-clusion about the desire for one's kindred is compatible with and even calls for a return to the earlier argument that love is of the useful or the good. It might appear, in other words, that a friend must be pleasant to be with as well as being useful or good. If so, however, Socrates must avoid the conse-quence that the kindred, or friend, is useless. He does this by distinguishing the kindred from what is like. He asks the boys whether they are willing to grant that what is akin is something other than the like. Claiming that they are drunk,

11. Cf. *Symposium* 192d2–e9.

as it were, from the argument, Socrates does not even bother to argue for this position. Had he wished to do so, he might have pointed to the kinship between opposites within a larger class of likes (for example, between men and women). Yet even without such elaboration, the tired boys—who forget the recent "denial" that friendly love is of the useful (cf. 221c5–d6)—are only too glad to follow Socrates' lead.

The demand that the kindred be useful, if it is to be a friend, prepares the way for Socrates' next question. Shall they posit, he asks, that what is good is akin to everyone, while what is bad is alien?[12] Now this suggestion, although it may seem abrupt, has in fact been prepared by Socrates' first conversation with Lysis. For there he argued that if Lysis became useful and good, then everyone would be friends and kinsmen (*oikeioi,* 210d2) to him. And since kinship has been seen to involve reciprocity, that earlier conclusion becomes equivalent to the claim that if Lysis were good he, also, would be akin (*oikeios*) to everyone. The present suggestion that *the* good— as distinct from someone good—is akin (*oikeion,* neuter) to everyone is simply a reinterpretation of that claim in the light of the intervening discussion of what it means to love the good. Yet there is a difficulty in this argument. Socrates' first conversation with Lysis had presupposed that everyone was aware, or could be made aware, of his own neediness, and that he was thus concerned above all with his own good. Yet we saw that this condition was not adequately fulfilled even in the case of Lysis himself. Moreover, Socrates has recently called attention to another and more immediately natural kinship—a kinship which draws beings of the same kind toward one

---

12. Cf. *Charmides* 163c3–6; *Symposium* 205e5–7. The word *oikeion* means, among other things, "fitting, suitable, or proper."

another. Accordingly, he now asks whether they should posit instead that what is bad is akin to the bad, and what is good is akin to the good, and what is neither good nor bad is akin to what is neither good nor bad.

Lysis and Menexenus both reply that in their opinion each is akin to each—that is, each is akin to its own kind—in the manner indicated by Socrates' second alternative. Their answer is hardly surprising, since the second alternative is the one which corresponds to our ordinary sense that there are various kinships among various kinds of beings. But Socrates objects that this alternative is an unacceptable account of the kindred, at least if the kindred are also friends. For it compels them to fall back into those assertions about friendship which they had rejected at first, namely that the unjust will be no less a friend to the unjust, and the bad no less a friend to the bad, than the good is a friend to the good (cf. 214b8–c5). One of the boys—it is probably the more persistent Menexenus (cf. 218c2–d1)—admits that they do seem to have fallen back into these assertions. But if, continues Socrates, they declare what is good and what is akin to be the same, then isn't only he who is good a friend, and a friend only to the good? "Very much so," is the reply.

Socrates' latest suggestion, that the good and the kindred are the same, is not precisely a return to the first alternative that the good is akin to everyone. For if the good were akin to everyone, then everyone would also be akin to the good. And if everyone were kindred (to the good), the claim that the kindred is the same as the good would be equivalent to saying that everyone is good. Yet as we have seen, there are many who are not even good enough to be aware of their own need for what is good (cf. 218a6–b1). The new result, however, that only the good is a friend to the good, does not itself seem satisfactory to Socrates. For he reminds the boys that "on this point, too, we supposed that we had refuted ourselves" (cf. 215a6–c2). He also asks them whether they remember that refutation, and they both reply that they do.

Here we are faced with the most striking perplexity of the dialogue. What are we to make of this assertion of friendship of the good for the good—an assertion which was once refuted and yet is now reintroduced as the dialogue's final positive claim? We should at least reconsider this claim, especially since Socrates' present objection is merely that they supposed (ōiometha, 222d8) they had refuted it, and not that they had done so in fact. In particular, the thesis of friendship between the good had been rejected at first on the grounds that the good, insofar as they are like each other, are useless to each other, and that insofar as they are good, they are self-sufficient and free of wants. Since the good, it was argued, are neither in want of each other when absent nor useful to each other when present, they would not treasure each other and accordingly they would not be one another's friends. Yet now, on the other hand, it has been admitted that those who are akin to each other, namely the good, are not necessarily like each other (222c1–3). And more importantly, it may no longer be possible to understand the self-sufficiency of the good as a simple freedom from wants. For we have seen that a being must be good for someone in order to be good (220c7–d7). Yet if there were a living being without wants, who could it be good for? We have argued that an eternally self-sufficient being could not be good for us humans, or at least not good enough to meet our needs, since it would always lack the wisdom about human things which we need for our well-being.

And if such a being, moreover, had no wants itself, it would hardly make sense to call it good for itself.[13] Only a being with wants and desires in need of being governed—by restraint, if restraint is appropriate, and by providing for their satisfaction, where to be satisfied would be better—can rightly be called useful or good for its own sake. A living being, in other words, must be at least vulnerable to evils in order to be good for itself. We conclude, then, that the self-sufficient beings who are good are necessarily composite beings. And for them to be good requires that they have, or have acquired, a share in those virtues which make them capable of benefiting themselves (and perhaps others). Despite the earlier denial of friendship between the good, this new understanding of their nature allows us to reopen the question whether such beings as these might be friends.

This understanding, however, of what it means to be good does not explain how the good can be friends, or friends in the fullest sense, to one another. In fact, if friends must be useful (222b8–c1), it would still seem impossible for the good to be one another's friends. For even if love of the useful were ever compatible with the love of one being for another, the self-sufficient have no use for others in order to meet their needs. Let us then interpret Socrates' latest suggestion to mean instead primarily that those who are good are friends to their share of what is good, and in that sense friends to themselves. For if we examine the suggestion closely, we note that it differs from the earlier version by the absence of any firm indication that both friends must be living beings (contrast 222d5–6 with 214e1 and 215b3–7; compare also 222e4). Therefore, we are free to interpret it as referring to the "kinship"[14] between

13. Cf. *Gorgias* 492e3–6.
14. Cf. *Gorgias* 506c3.

beings who are sufficient or good for themselves, on the one hand, and their good—their virtue (*aretē*), along with whatever other goods become theirs—on the other. Their share of what is good could be appropriate or akin to such beings, and thus pleasant, and at the same time useful to them, as we have just seen. Accordingly, they would love it, even though it was already in a sense "theirs." They would love to continue to have a share in it, in the future as well as in the present (contrast 218a2–4). Still, however, the force of this suggestion is weakened by the fact that it seems to leave no room for reciprocity. Reciprocal love has been said to characterize the love of the kindred, and yet that which is good does not itself love. So how could it have any "love" for that aspect of composite beings which is in need of what is good? Yet though the good does not of course love in the strict sense (cf. 212d7–8), it is nevertheless in "need" of a needy being in order for it to be useful or good (cf. 220c7–d7). And that good which is not good for someone is incomplete; while it might still be somehow beautiful, it has not yet come into its own.[15] Accordingly, there is a reciprocal dependence between the neediness and the goodness of a self-sufficient being. The being who is good, we can say, insofar as he is deficient, is a friend who loves his share of what is good, and insofar as it is good, it is a friend which "accepts the friendship" (cf. 219a4) of itself as a living and needy being.[16] In this way, then, despite the earlier refutation, we can understand how the good might be a friend to the good.[17]

In examining this final claim about the good as friend, we

15. Cf. Leo Strauss, *Socrates and Aristophanes* (New York, 1966), p. 296.

16. Consider *Alcibiades I* 133c4–6.

17. Concerning the relationship between love of the good and love of oneself, see also pp. 174–176 above.

must also reflect upon Socrates' sudden silence, in the last stages of his argument, about those intermediates who are neither good nor bad. Or is his silence only apparent? Perhaps Socrates has not entirely disregarded the intermediates, since some of them might not be distinct from some among the good. A healthy body, at any rate, and a good soul are "themselves in themselves" simply body and soul, which as such are neither good nor bad (cf. 220c4–5). Similarly, others who are good might also be beings which in themselves are neither good nor bad. This would be true, at least, of those who had become good in the course of time.[18] Beings who were not always good, and who therefore are not likely to remain good forever, are not necessarily good. Therefore, although they may be in a sense perfectible, they are "themselves in themselves" neither good nor bad. And among such beings are all those—if there are any—whose temporary or lasting self-sufficiency includes the perfection of wisdom (cf. 218a2–4). In other words, any living being whose goodness included such wisdom as men merely strive for would be, like us, "itself in itself" neither good nor bad. And only such an intermediate being could become a wise and good friend to its share of what is good.

There still remains, of course, the question of how such self-sufficient beings might be related to one another. Might not some of them, at least, be one another's friends, if only in a limited sense? For even without needing one another, and without longing for one another in order to become whole (cf. 215b4), they might still, being kindred, desire and enjoy one another's company. And if this were so, their friendly feeling for one another might be in a sense exemplary. For

18. Cf. *Protagoras* 345b8–2.

their affection would be free of the illusions which deceive the most generous or erotic of human friends. And it would also be free of the selfishness at the root of all human desire for useful friends. Therefore, some of the self-sufficiently good might enjoy with each other among the purest, if not the deepest, of "friendships." Moreover, if any of them have become good in the course of time, they might also be akin to others of their kind who are still becoming so. And their affection toward these "youths," though conditional upon the others' desire and ability to improve, would be similarly pure. Indeed, we could not fully understand Socrates' own fondness for the young—though he of course never claims to be self-sufficient or good—without taking such an affection into account.[19]

19. Cf. *Alcibiades I* 131c5–d7.

The Ending of the Dialogue
(222d8–223b8)

We cannot be certain whether the interpretation given here does justice to Socrates' renewed assertion that only the good is friend to the good. Rather, as we have seen, Socrates dismisses the whole suggestion without even an argument. He allows the mention of an alleged previous refutation to stand in the way of any rethinking such as has been attempted here. And now, instead of pursuing the argument, he suggests that they can make nothing more of it. Accordingly, he says that he merely wants to do as those who are wise in the law courts do, to count up all that has been said.

Socrates' summation is a restatement of various suggestions that had been proposed, and apparently rejected, concerning who are friends. He mentions those who are loved, those who love, those who are alike, those who are unlike, those who are good, and those who are kindred. As for any other suggestions that might have been made, he claims that he doesn't remember the rest because of their multitude. If nothing among these is a friend, he concludes, then he no longer knows what to say. Socrates differs from those who are wise in the law courts by ending his summation with an acknowledgment of failure. But like them, he has not given a precise or exhaustive summary of the earlier suggestions. His most important omissions are of those who both love and are loved, on the one hand (cf. 213c6–7), and of the intermediate beings in their friendly relation to the good, on the other (cf. 216c2–3; 220b7). In other words, his omissions recall our attention to the main question which had been raised in the first explicit discussion of who are friends: what is the relation between friendship in the ordinary sense, which requires that the friends both love and be loved, and the friendly disposition, without any desire to be loved, which men have toward the good which they pursue? Now conceivably, Socrates hoped that someone present might notice his omissions and thus help him to renew the inquiry into this central question. At any rate, he reports in his narration that while giving this summary he already had in mind to set in motion someone among the older fellows.

Socrates was prevented, however, from continuing the discussion by the unexpected arrival of the attendants of Menexenus and Lysis. The two tutors had evidently gone away, leaving the boys unattended, at some time (since 208c3) during the earlier conversations. But now they returned and brought with them the boys' brothers. According to Socrates, they approached like some daemons (*hōsper daimones tines,* 223a2), calling to the boys and bidding them to leave for home. These two "daemons" are like Socrates' own *daimonion* in opposing what he intended to do, rather than urging him forward to anything.[1] Yet Socrates did not yield to these two men as willingly as he would have yielded to his own daemonic voice. Even though it was already late (223a5), he and the boys, along with those who had been standing around listening, tried to drive them away. Socrates, then, directed or at least assisted Lysis and Menexenus in a rebellion against the guardians appointed by their fathers. Yet despite his and the

---

1. Cf. *Apology of Socrates* 31d2–4.

boys' resistance, the attendants paid no heed to them. They merely showed some irritation, and kept calling out with their somewhat foreign accent. In the opinion of Socrates and the boys, moreover, the attendants had been drinking at the festival, and so there seemed to be no way to approach them. We understand by this, in the first place, that they were too drunk to be open to coaxing or to persuasion. And second, although they were outnumbered by Socrates' circle, their shouting could have attracted the attention of enough adults to subdue both him and the recalcitrant boys. Recognizing, therefore, that they were defeated, Socrates and the boys broke up (*dielusamen*, 223b3) their group.

This final scene shows emphatically how Socrates' desire to be together with the young brought him into conflict with his fellow Athenians. His fondness for the young, together with his questioning nature, led him to become an enemy of sorts to that primary friendship, and primary authority, which is the family. He threatened the authority enjoyed by fathers over their sons. Yet Socrates' defeat in this scene suggests further that his threat to parental rule may not have been so very great. This evidence in deed of Socrates' weakness contrasts with his early discussion with Lysis (207d5–210d8), where it was concluded that a wise man would supplant fathers and all others and become ruler over everyone. But the conclusion there presupposed unusual and extreme circumstances, and it had assumed, more importantly, that the wise were willing to serve everyone as their rulers. Neither of these conditions was fulfilled on this particular occasion. Accordingly, Socrates could not even contrive, despite his "wisdom in erotic matters" (cf. 206a1), to be left alone in peace for very long with his companions. Even together with his supporters, Socrates was not nearly a match for those who would maintain the

lawful rule of fathers over their sons. Therefore, after a show
of struggle, he soon resigned himself to the temporary freedom he had enjoyed with the two boys while their attendants
had been away. He was not so foolish as to continue a hopeless
effort to keep the boys with himself.

As Lysis and Menexenus are departing, however, Socrates
does call out to them some final words. He claims that he, an
old man, and they have become ridiculous. "For these fellows," he explains, "will say as they go away that we suppose
we're one another's friends—for I also put myself among you
—but we have not yet been able to discover what he who is a
friend is." Socrates' parting words are meant to warn the boys
that they cannot know themselves to be friends, as distinct
from merely supposing that they are, without knowing what
a friend is.[2] He may also wish to encourage them to continue
inquiring. But we should observe that Socrates does not say,
in regard to himself, that he even supposes he is the boys'
friend; he merely claims that the others will say so as they go
away. Though he may want the two boys to feel comfortable
with him and to think of him as their friend, he himself in all
likelihood resists the temptation so easily to suppose that they
are his (cf. 212a4–7). One sign of his successful resistance is
that he can speak of his forced separation from his young
"friends" as no greater an evil than the occasion for ridicule.

2. Cf. *Charmides* 176a6–b1.

The Pohlenz-von Arnim
Controversy about the *Lysis*

The question which divided Max Pohlenz and Hans von
Arnim in their controversy about the *Lysis* is a perennial one,
rooted in the dialogue itself and in the very nature of friendship. It is better to see this question in sharp focus, as they did,
than to evade it through facile attempts at harmonization.
Pohlenz and von Arnim differed over the relationship between
the *Lysis* and the *Symposium* or, more directly stated, between
friendship (*philia*) and erotic love (*erōs*). Did Plato believe, as
Pohlenz thought he did, that they are kindred phenomena, or
did he, along with von Arnim, consider them to be "two fundamentally different dispositions of the soul and relations between men."[1] One can state this same question more precisely
by asking about the highest friendship. Was Pohlenz right in
arguing that no Platonic friendship is free of "the element of
striving and desire"?[2] Or did Plato believe, as von Arnim contends that he did, that there is a unique case of perfect friendship, possible only between virtuous men who love (*philousi*)
each other "with pure love, free of all desire stemming from
need, and which alone in the highest and truest sense deserves

1. The phrase is from Ulrich von Wilamowitz-Möllendorff, *Platon,* 2
vols. (Berlin, 1920), II, 68, who follows von Arnim on this point. All
translations from the German are my own.
2. Max Pohlenz, book review in *Göttingische gelehrte Anzeigen* 5 (May
1916), 254. Cf. Pohlenz, *Aus Platos Werdezeit* (Berlin, 1913), p. 367.

to be called friendship"?[3] Pohlenz, citing *Lysis* 215a4–c2, argues against this that perfectly good men, being free of need, would be incapable of friendship. Underlying von Arnim's contention, on the other hand, is his more fundamental view that the main purpose of the *Lysis* is to show that the Good is loved "as such and for its own sake" and that desire or need cannot be considered as a necessary element in this highest love, which "rather would continue, even if we possessed [the Good]."[4] From this source von Arnim derives the possibility of perfect, unerotic friendship between men, for "he who loves the Good as such and himself possesses it, i.e. is good, loves it also in other men who possess it."[5]

Only gradually did the dispute between Pohlenz and von Arnim come to center on the *Lysis*. Originally, the two scholars differed over the Platonic question as it appeared in the nineteenth and early twentieth centuries—the question of whether the chronological order of Plato's writings mirrors his own philosophic development. Pohlenz's book *Aus Platos Werdezeit* (Berlin, 1913) is an investigation of the early dialogues in which he assumes, as did most scholars of his generation, that such a mirroring is evident. In a long footnote (pp. 330–332) he takes issue with von Arnim as a representative of the opposing position, which he illustrates by citing the following programmatic statement of von Arnim: "When Plato founded his school and came forward as a teacher of philosophy, then, we may confidently believe, he already saw the outlines of his world-view clearly and distinctly before

3. Hans von Arnim, *Platos Jugenddialoge und die Entstehungszeit des Phaidros* (Leipzig, 1914), p. 62.

4. Von Arnim, "Platos *Lysis,*" *Rheinisches Museum für Philologie* 71 (1916). Also, von Arnim, *Platos Jugenddialoge,* p. 58.

5. Von Arnim, *Platos Jugenddialoge,* p. 62.

him. . . . We must try, insofar as it is possible, to defend the unity in this sense of Plato's teaching against those who speculate about his development." Pohlenz warns, by contrast, of a "harmonistic tendency" in von Arnim's work.

In the following year, von Arnim systematically challenged the prevailing view, and Pohlenz in particular, in a book entitled *Platos Jugenddialoge und die Entstehungszeit des Phaidros* (Leipzig, 1914). His polemic against Pohlenz begins with the second paragraph of the foreword to his book.

> I could not have found for my book a beautiful and stimulating title such as "Aus Platos Werdezeit." Surely, the task presents itself, among others, of bringing forward into the field—against the genetic conception of Platonic writing, which is effectively expressed in this title and which has been ruling in Germany since K. F. Hermann —the relative justification of the conception represented by Schleiermacher, which finds a methodical-didactic system in Plato's writing and in the order of his writings.[6]

In this foreword, von Arnim expresses his gratitude to Paul Shorey's *The Unity of Plato's Thought* (Chicago, 1903) for steering him away from the pitfalls of the genetic view, and in particular from "the danger of seeking, and naturally also of finding, contradictions between various writings of the philosopher which prove to be, if one enters deeper into Plato's intention and his way of thinking, only apparent contradictions."[7] He argues that an attempt such as Pohlenz's to see

6. Ibid., p. iii
7. Ibid., pp. iii-iv.

Plato's own philosophic development in the sequence of his earlier writings could never succeed, because these writings move "in a unified circle of thought." "They do not," he writes, "mirror a Platonic 'time of development (*Werdezeit*).' Rather one could say that they are intended to grant a time of development to the reader."[8]

Pohlenz had asserted, in a chapter entitled *"Lysis* und *Symposion,"* that the *Lysis* was written soon after the *Phaedrus*. He argued that it grew from the same series of speculations about *erōs,* and in particular from the question whether *erōs* is grounded in likeness or opposition. He also claimed that the *Lysis* supplies one important and deliberate correction of the *Phaedrus*. For the assertion in the *Phaedrus* (255b) that "it has not been destined that bad ever be a friend to bad or that good not be a friend to good" (*ou gar dēpote heimartai kakon kakōi philon oud'agathon mē philon agathōi einai*), is directly contradicted by the *Lysis* (215a), which says that the good, as such, cannot be friends.[9] In all friendship there is the element of striving and desire, from which the good as good are free. This thought leads directly, according to Pohlenz, "to the fundamental view of the *Symposium*."[10]

Pohlenz's attempt to understand the *Lysis* as an intermediate stage between the *Phaedrus* and the *Symposium* is challenged by von Arnim in his chapter on the *Lysis*. Von Arnim contends, instead, in agreement with his earlier conclusions from stylometric evidence, that the *Lysis* is earlier than both of these other dialogues. In his view it is a mistake in any case to interpret the *Lysis* from an erotic perspective, and he claims

8. Ibid., p. v.
9. Pohlenz, *Aus Platos Werdezeit,* p. 368.
10. Pohlenz, book review in *Göttingische gelehrte Anzeigen,* 5:254.

that *erōs* plays only a peripheral role in it.[11]

Pohlenz's response to these assertions appeared two years later in a review article of von Arnim's book. Pohlenz challenges von Arnim's "unitarianism" and argues again that it conceals methodological dangers no less grave than those of the genetic view. Many of his criticisms are directed against von Arnim's reading of the *Lysis,* and he contends that von Arnim entirely misinterprets the dialogue. This misinterpretation, he argues, stems from the fact that von Arnim "does not interpret the dialogue simply on its own terms, but on the basis of conceptions which he gathers from other Platonic writings he believes that he can ascertain what Plato could and could not have seriously meant."[12] Most especially, Pohlenz challenges von Arnim's key assertion—which contradicts *Lysis* 215a–c, and is supported chiefly by the already cited passage from the *Phaedrus* (255b)—that there can be a friendship between the good which is distinct in kind from those friendships bound up with desire.[13] In opposition, he also offers his own positive interpretation of the dialogue.[14]

Von Arnim soon replied with an article ("Platos *Lysis*") defending his position and reemphasizing the decisive importance of the fact that the Good is loved for its own sake and not because of any need or desire external to itself. It is on this basis, according to von Arnim, that perfectly good men, that

11. Von Arnim, *Platos Jugenddialoge,* p. 40. See also *Sprachlichen Forschungen zur Chronologie der platonischen Dialoge—Sitzungsberichtungen der Wiener Akademie,* vol. 169.

12. Pohlenz, book review *Göttingische gelehrte Anzeigen,* 5:260.

13. Cf. Pohlenz, "Nochmals Platos *Lysis,*" *Nachrichten von der Königlichen Gesellschaft der Wissenschaften zu Göttingen, Philologisch-historische Klasse,* 1917, p. 588.

14. Pohlenz, book review in *Göttingische gelehrte Anzeigen,* 5:258.

is, those who possess the Good, can also love each other with a love that is free of desire. Von Arnim also accuses Pohlenz of violating his own methodological principles by interpreting the *Lysis* in the light of the *Symposium*. In particular, he claims that Pohlenz's positive interpretation of the *Lysis* is a borrowing of theories from Aristophanes' speech and from Diotima's speech, although these two speeches are far from equal in philosophic importance and are not in direct relation to each other.[15]

The following year, Pohlenz replied with a paper entitled "Nochmals Platos *Lysis*." In this paper Pohlenz makes some important concessions to von Arnim but reasserts his main criticism that the latter's notion of perfect friendship comes from elsewhere in Plato, and especially from Aristotle, rather than from the *Lysis* itself. He also restates his positive interpretation and adheres more strictly this time to his rule that the *Lysis* first be interpreted on its own terms before its teaching is compared with what we read elsewhere in Plato. Several years later, Pohlenz published a review of Wilamowitz's *Platon*,[16] in which he concedes that he had erred in dating the *Phaedrus* before the *Lysis* but reaffirms his fundamental contention that the *Lysis* is closely related to the *Symposium*. In his opinion Platonic friendship, being grounded in our feeling of lack or imperfection, is closely akin to erotic love (*erōs*).

I am inclined to side with Pohlenz's stand that friendship is inseparable from *erōs*, or rather from deficiency. I side with Pohlenz despite the fact that his notion of the evolution of Plato's thought leaves him open to valid criticism. Moreover, his insistence on interpreting a dialogue on its own terms, and

15. Von Arnim, "Platos *Lysis*," pp. 369, 371.
16. *Göttingische gelehrte Anzeigen,* No. 1–3 (1921), pp. 1–30.

as an artistic whole, leads him greatly to underestimate the difficulties in finding the unity among the several parts within the *Lysis* itself. And von Arnim is right to contend that Pohlenz's positive solution to the problems of the dialogue looks like a mixture, fundamentally lacking in clarity, of the two main speeches from the *Symposium*. Despite these failings, however, my account of this debate will use Pohlenz's arguments as the beginning for a critical analysis of von Arnim's reading of the *Lysis*.

Both Pohlenz and von Arnim agree that the aporetic conclusion of the dialogue—Socrates' apparent ignorance about what a friend is—does not mean that Plato had no positive teaching about friendship. A major obstacle, however, to our finding a positive teaching is the contradiction between two alternative accounts, both of which are introduced by Socrates and both of which he refutes. The first of these accounts is that friendship exists between likes, who—since the bad are unstable, and not even alike to themselves—turn out to be equivalent to the good. Thus, as Socrates says (*Lysis* 214d5–6), "he who is good is a friend to the good—he alone to him alone." This thesis reappears, somewhat surprisingly, at the end of the dialogue (222d6) in the guise of Socrates' last attempt to save the assertion that the friend is one's own, or the kindred (*to oikeion.*) For it appears at the end that only the Good is one's own and that only those who are good are really akin to, and friends of, each other. Yet as Socrates there says, "Even on this point we thought we had refuted ourselves." And here is the difficulty. For Socrates had indeed already refuted the claim that only the good can be friends. He had done this by arguing that the good, insofar as they are good, are self-sufficient, hence free of wants and needs, and thus even incapable of friendship (215a4–c2). The denial of this thesis of friendship between the good prepared the way for the alternative account, subsequently developed at length, that only those beings who are neither good nor bad are friends of the Good (216e7–217a2). In other words, "friendship" is the striving of beings like us, who are in between (*metaxu*) good and bad, in pursuit of the Good. According to this second account, the Good which we love does not have to be a living being, and there is no necessity that it love us in return. Moreover, according to this understanding of friendship, if we ever were to become perfectly good (that is, to possess the Good), we would no longer love the Good, since we would no longer need it. Those who are already wise, for example, no longer love wisdom or philosophize (cf. 218a3); only those do so who are not yet either wholly wise or wholly ignorant. Hence it does appear that friendship, or love of the Good, depends on the presence of *some* ignorance or evil. This second account, however, is also denied by Socrates, for he finds it strange that the Good is dear, or a friend, to us only because of some evil. Even if evils were to disappear, he argues, there would still be friendship. And after an important detour, Socrates returns to his assertion that friendship unites only the good with each other. But then, to repeat, he reminds the boys that they thought they had refuted this assertion, and so he abandons the argument. Thus we have a perfect friendship, independent of wants and needs, which seems not to exist, and an imperfect one, admittedly dependent on need, which fails to account for the whole phenomenon of friendship.

Von Arnim's interpretation of the *Lysis* is an attempt to discover a unified teaching about friendship from the wreckage of these two accounts. His single most controversial assertion—the assertion that initiates the whole debate—is that Socrates did not seriously mean to deny the possibility of friendship between the good. Now Socrates surely does say that the good cannot be friends (215a), but von Arnim does not take this denial seriously. "To see Plato's real opinion in this thesis, which goes even further than the self-sufficiency of the Stoic wise man, would be a great naïvety."[17] And he explains the reappearance late in the dialogue of the claim that the good are friends as a sign that this is Plato's genuine opinion. In von Arnim's view, Plato believed not only that friendship is possible between the good, but also that theirs is more truly friendship than those "friendships" which depend on the needs and wants of imperfect beings. And he claims to find evidence in support of this position in Socrates' first statement of the thesis that the good are friends. "He who is good," says Socrates, "is a friend to the good—he alone to him alone—while he who is bad never comes into *true* friendship with either the good or the bad" (214d5–7, italics mine; cf. also 220a–b). Here von Arnim sees a hint of Aristotle's complete friendship, which is limited to those who are good and which, while not being the only friendship, is the only *true* friendship. And he claims that Socrates' denial of friendship between the good applies only to the inferior kinds of "friendship," and not to the true one.

Pohlenz, however, believes that Plato "is serious throughout [the dialogue] about the denial of friendship between the perfectly good."[18] He calls attention, moreover, to von Ar-

17. Von Arnim, *Platos Jugenddialoge,* p. 46.

18. Pohlenz, book review in *Göttingische gelehrte Anzeigen,* 5:254. In his denial of friendship between the good, Pohlenz is open to the possibility—in fact, he is inclined to believe—that such perfect beings do not exist on earth. We humans, who can be friends, must be content in his opinion if we are among those "intermediate" beings who strive to be good. On this point also, von Arnim disagrees. (See Pohlenz, "Nochmals Platos *Lysis,*"

nim's lack of textual support for his assertion to the contrary. Von Arnim's main Platonic evidence for friendship between the good consists of a single sentence from the *Phaedrus* (255b1–2), an overall notion about friendship in the *Republic,* and a few lines from the *Laws* (716c). But Pohlenz denies, and rightly, that this evidence is relevant. For it is clear from the contexts that only the passage in the *Lysis,* as distinct from the others, is concerned with the perfectly good, with those who are good in the strictest sense of the term. Only these beings, and not the guardian class of the *Republic,* for example (*Republic* 387d), are wholly self-sufficient and incapable for that reason of being friends.[19] And as for Socrates' use of the phrase "true friendship" (214d7), Pohlenz interprets it merely as his way of stressing his disagreement with the vulgar view, according to which those who are bad can indeed be friends. And Pohlenz denies that friendship between the good is being called true, as distinguished from pretended, friendship. In his view, no distinction is being made among types of friendship; the so-called friendship of the bad is, strictly speaking, no friendship at all.

On this last point, however, Pohlenz appears to have gone too far. Socrates' statement that the bad can have no *true* friendship is the dialogue's only reference to true friendship.

---

p. 567, and von Arnim, "Platos *Lysis,*" p. 376.) There is an apparent connection between the two men's positions on this question and their attitudes toward the possibility of "perfect" friendship. For it would seem to be misanthropic to claim that men can be good without also asserting that such good men can have each other as friends. In other words, both Pohlenz and von Arnim allow that the best among men can be friends of each other.

19. Ibid., pp. 253–254. Pohlenz, "Nochmals Platos *Lysis,*" pp. 564–565.

And such unique usages can be extremely important in a Platonic dialogue. Moreover, Socrates could hardly be so paradoxical as to maintain seriously that bad men can have no friends in any sense of the word. There is a distinction among types of friendship, and perhaps indeed the friendship of those who are good is to be understood as the only true kind. Von Arnim might well be right on this point. But at all events Pohlenz is correct in the decisive respect when he insists that friendship between the good is shown in the sequel to be impossible. If von Arnim is right that there is a distinct "true friendship" between only the good, this would seem to imply, according to the *Lysis,* that true or complete reciprocal friendship is an impossible dream. But it would not affect Socrates' argument that there can be no friendship between those who are perfectly good. This argument should not be dismissed without an answer, but von Arnim fails even to attempt one.

Von Arnim, then, seems to have been mistaken in trying to sever the connection between friendship and neediness or want. There is no evidence in the *Lysis,* or elsewhere in Plato, for his notion of a possible friendship which is unrelated to desire (*epithymia*) and to erotic love (*erōs*). In fairness to him, however, we must now turn to the second half of the debate, to the assertion which von Arnim himself considered the cornerstone of his argument, his assertion about the Good. According to von Arnim, the fundamental dogma of the *Lysis* is that "the Good is akin to everyone, and the bad is alien" (*to agathon oikeion panti, to de kakon allotrion,* 222c4). In other words, all men originally love and strive after the Good as that which properly belongs to them and which they have a claim to possess. To be sure, admits von Arnim, this love is most often bound together with desire. But it is fundamental for him that desire and *erōs* cannot be considered the grounds of love of the Good, since "the good, finally, who already possess the Good, do not cease on that account to love it. They love it as 'their own' (oikeion), as a possession from which they do not want to part."[20] This understanding of love of the Good is von Arnim's foundation for his thesis about complete friendship. For "whoever loves the Good as such and possesses it himself, i.e. is good, loves it also in other men who possess it, with a pure love—free of all desire stemming from need—which alone in the highest and most proper sense deserves to be named philia."[21] What is most important here is that von Arnim's understanding of the Good enables him to reconcile the two accounts of friendship which have been mentioned previously. Though they are both apparently refuted, they are both true if rightly understood. That to agathon oikeion panti (the Good is akin to everyone) can be considered a more comprehensive version of the thesis that the Good is a friend to those who are neither good nor bad. According to this view, even bad men once loved the Good, but since they have become ignorant of their need for it, they have lost their love. Then also, those who are neither good nor bad, those who do not lose sight of their need for the Good, do love it and desire to possess it. This intermediate love is naturally related to desire. But finally, since the Good is a real object and not just the goal of our striving, those who become good, as some men do, continue to love it as their own (oikeion). This last stage of love is free of any appetite or desire. And from this love there flows that reciprocal friendship between the good which is the only true friendship among men. Thus, von Arnim's interpretation of the state-

20. Von Arnim, Platos Jugenddialoge, p. 62; compare p. 49.
21. Ibid., p. 62.

ment *to agathon oikeion panti* allows both for an appetitive love, which is inseparable from desire and striving, and also for a love that is free from these deficiencies.

By this interpretation von Arnim appears to have overcome the contradiction between the dialogue's two main accounts of friendship. But the detailed elaboration that Socrates gives of the second account raises further difficulties, and it seems to confirm the earlier denial of friendship between good men. For Socrates' argument, in its developed form, is that the being who is neither good nor bad is a friend of the good, for the sake of a further good, and because of the presence of an evil. This means, to take Socrates' own example, that a man who is sick but who knows that he is sick becomes a friend of the doctor, for the sake of his health, and because of his disease. In other words, there appear to be three conditions placed on friendship with the good. First, the one who loves the good must be neither good nor bad, but rather an intermediate being who strives to make the good his own. Second, the particular good must be loved for the sake of (*heneka*) a further good, and so on and so on until his love terminates in the Good itself, which is the one ultimate goal, or "Finalgrund" (final cause), of all friendship. And third, the good must be loved because of (*dia*) the presence of some evil that afflicts the one who loves. The evils which trouble us, and which we try to escape, are the "Realgrund" (real cause) that gives the first impetus to our love for what is good. It should be noted that the assertion of this "real cause" and of this "final cause" as conditions for friendly love goes together with the denial that those who are good can be friends. For a perfectly good man would be free of evils, and he would no longer be striving for any further good.

According to von Arnim, however, Plato does not ultimately intend to place any of these conditions on the love of the Good. Though von Arnim never denies, of course, that imperfect beings do love the Good, he does deny—in keeping with his earlier assertions—that this love is limited to such beings. Furthermore, he goes on to claim that the notions of the Good as the "final cause" of love, and of evils as its "real cause," are not really Platonic ones. Rather, he claims, they are theories of another philosopher which Socrates will eliminate by showing them to be absurd.[22] The Good, according to von Arnim, cannot be considered as the final goal of our desire, since in that case it might be merely the product of imagination. What it is, rather, is Plato's Idea of the Good (at least in nascent form), which exists as the real object of our loving. Von Arnim considers the real existence of the Idea of the Good to be the core of Platonism as it manifests itself in the *Lysis*. For him, this is the fundamental fact. The Good cannot be accounted for in terms of anything beyond itself. And in particular, it is the real object and not merely the goal of love.

> To show the Good as an object of love means for Plato to show it as real, because the object of love must have existence outside of and prior to love itself; the Good as the goal of love's striving is immanent in this striving as a mere conception in the mind; and if it is realized through this striving, it thus wins its existence through this striving for the first time. As the goal to be realized through striving, the Good could belong only to this spatial-temporal world, of whose "becoming" all the effects of our striving comprise a part: as the object of love, the

22. Ibid., p. 50.

Good can only be a reality which exists as Idea (*ideell Reales*). To prove that this second alternative is correct is the main philosophical intention of the *Lysis*.[23]

Yet even if the Good should be an object rather than a goal of love, the question of the "real cause" still remains. One can still ask whether there is any external cause, aside from its intrinsic attractiveness, of love for the Good. Might not only those love it who are beset by evils which they desire to escape? But von Arnim believes that this is manifestly untrue.

> We see at first glance that the "Realgrund" of our love for the Good and Beautiful cannot, in Plato's view, be the bad, but only the Good and Beautiful themselves. . . . According to Plato, surely, the Good is something positive, not the mere negation of evil. Were it however loved only because of the bad, then its own essence would have to be thought of as purely negative, just as Epicurus determines the essence of his highest good as the "removal of everything painful."[24]

Thus the Good is loved itself for its own sake, without ulterior motives and without prior instigation. This love of the Good is free of any desire which stems from need. From von Arnim's perspective, the elimination of false "final" and "real" causes is a purification of our understanding of friendly love in order that we might see it in all its simplicity. This purified understanding, in turn, provides a basis for the claim

23. Von Arnim, "Platos *Lysis*," pp. 381–382; cf. von Arnim, *Platos Jugenddialoge*, p. 53.

24. Von Arnim, *Platos Jugenddialoge*, p. 54.

that even and especially the good are capable of such love, both love of the Good as their own (*oikeion*) and love of each other as good.

Von Arnim has much stronger textual support for this part of his argument than he did before. For Socrates does indeed assert that the Good itself is what is really dear, or the real friend, and that our love of it has no "final cause" beyond itself (220b6–7). He also goes on to deny that evils are the cause of friendship by showing that there would still be friends even if there were no longer any evils. Hence, he argues, there must be some other cause, besides evils, of friendship and love (221b8–d2). The evidence that the one who loves does not have to be an intermediate being, one who is neither good nor bad, is far less direct. But it is true that the final stage of the argument reconsiders both the bad and the good, along with the intermediates, as possible friends. And the conversation does indeed lead back to the puzzling conclusion that the good can be a friend to the good (222c3–d8).

In his response to this section of von Arnim's argument, Pohlenz says that he cannot believe Plato would have introduced a "final" and a "real" cause of friendship only to have them eliminated. Yet his own first discussion of the notion of "final cause" suffered, according to his later admission, from an insufficient appreciation of von Arnim's claim that the Good is a real object which is loved for its own sake. Despite his recantation, however, Pohlenz continues to insist in his second article that the notion of the Good as "final cause" is valid as it applies to our subordinate loves. In all the loves and friendships of our lives, we strive, if only unconsciously, for possession of the Good. It is, according to Pohlenz, this unconscious desire for the absolute Good which draws us to particular goods and to particular human beings.[25] Here we must step back for a moment, for this is a hard assertion. If it is true, then each of us, in his relations with others, desires above all to possess the Good for himself. We would use other men—to put it simply—as means in our pursuit of this end. We would not love any other living beings for themselves alone or for their own sake; presumably, then, we would receive no such love from others. We would be unable to love others as we love ourselves and as we want ourselves to be loved. The harshness of this thesis is hardly mitigated by the recognition that in our use of others we could be most generous and kind and that our love might seem at times—to others and even to ourselves—to be free of self-regard. For it would still remain true that we lived with others by using and being used.

Von Arnim's view of perfect friendship between the good compels him to deny the notion of a "final cause" which entails these consequences. Yet on what basis can he do this? Let us grant that the Good, or "what is really a friend," or "what is really dear," is not loved for the sake of anything else (220b6–7). Let us also admit for purposes of discussion that men are not condemned to imperfection, that they can become perfectly good by possessing the Good as their own. We can even perhaps allow, despite *Lysis* 218a2–b3, that those who are good continue to love the Good as their own (if only on the grounds that they would never want to lose it). But on what basis can von Arnim be confident that such good men also love each other with generous friendly love? What is this Good which causes those who possess it to overflow with love

25. Pohlenz, book review in *Göttingische gelehrte Anzeigen*, 5:255–256. Also Pohlenz, "Nochmals Platos *Lysis*," pp. 570–571.

of other good men? Surely it is not like health of the body, which Socrates had used as his first example of a good (219a). For men who are healthy in this way do not necessarily love those others who are like themselves. But the "Idea of the Good" is more probably something whose "possession" gives rise instead to health of the soul. Maybe good men are those with healthy souls. Yet do we know enough about health of the soul to know its consequences for human life? Socrates— whom von Arnim presumably considers to have been a good man with a healthy soul—did, of course, search for a good friend (*Lysis* 211d6–e8). But he seems to have done it in the *gymnasia* and to have enjoyed the company of promising youths more than that of other mature men. This feature of Socrates' life is especially evident in the *Lysis*. Did Socrates choose to spend so much of his time with the young only in despair of finding a truly good adult to be his friend? If we cannot find record of complete friendship in Socrates' life, where in Plato can we hope to find it? We are compelled, therefore, to reaffirm that von Arnim has failed to show how, according to Plato, good men can love each other with a love that is free of want and need. (This is not to say, however, that Pohlenz has provided an adequate account of why human beings are friends of each other.)

As for the "real cause," Pohlenz agrees with von Arnim that Plato could not have regarded the presence of evils as a true cause of love of the Good. "According to Plato's whole world-view that is impossible."[26] And indeed, Socrates himself seems to say as much at *Lysis* 221c. But Pohlenz denies von Arnim's contention that a "real cause," distinct from the Good itself, is entirely dismissed. In his view the "presence of

26. Pohlenz, "Nochmals Platos *Lysis,*" p. 572.

an evil" is replaced by *endeia,* or "the feeling of a lack," as such a cause. He argues, moreover, that this suggestion is not incompatible with Platonism. "The thought would be intolerable for Plato that the real existence of the bad is that which first calls forth the striving for the Good and conditions its value. On the other hand it is, from the Platonic point of view at least, not unthinkable in advance that it is a feeling of lack, of imperfection, which gives us the external impetus to this striving."[27] Pohlenz is asking us, then, to consider the question whether lack, or rather the feeling of a lack, should perhaps be understood as the true "real cause" through which our love of the Good is awakened and sustained. More broadly stated, is Pohlenz correct to assert the importance of a "real cause," other than the Good itself, in the true account of friendly love? Can the account of love of the Good be purified of such a "real cause" and of those imperfections which it implies?

According to von Arnim, the hypothesis that *endeia* (lack) is the "real cause" of love of the Good belongs to a subsection of the dialogue in which Plato criticizes the subjectivistic theories of Aristippus and other philosophers. Von Arnim thinks that Plato uses this section to contrast his conviction that the Good is the ultimate source of value, which is loved for its own sake, with the most extreme alternative. The extreme alternative is that the "good" is merely the object of a wanting man's desire (*epithymia*), and that it has value only for him, and only because and only so long as he desires it (cf. 221d3–4). Simply stated, the question is this: "Is, then, the Good good because it is desired or is it rather desired because it is good?" Now for von Arnim, "it is clear how Plato must

27. Ibid., p. 574.

answer this question in accordance with the intellectualistic tendency of his thought. For him, the main thing was to show that values are realities objectively contained in the nature of things."[28] The goodness of the Good is, for von Arnim, the cause and not the consequence of human desire; the Good itself is a real object which is the only real cause of love. According to von Arnim, Plato indicates the primacy of the Good by suggesting that it would still be valued and loved even if all evils were to disappear from the world. Therefore, although there is indeed a desire, related to erotic love (*erōs*), to possess the missing Good, this desire is the consequence of the Good and not the cause of our loving it. Moreover, the Good is loved without desire by those good men who already possess it. And they alone can be true friends, and friends only to each other. Here, according to von Arnim, is the teaching of the *Lysis* in a nutshell. But von Arnim thinks that Plato did not want to end the dialogue on this note of certainty, but chose instead to elicit these thoughts from the reader. Accordingly, and in order to present the extreme alternative, Plato added the subsection in which "lack" replaces "the bad" as the "real cause" of friendship, and in which "the kindred" replaces "the Good" as the object of desire and love. According to von Arnim, the presupposition of this subsection—that friendship is "desire for one's kindred"—is alien to Plato. And the notion that "lack" is the "real cause" of love, far from being an aspect of the true account of friendship, belongs only in this unplatonic context.[29]

I am persuaded by von Arnim's claim that the notion of "lack" belongs, at least initially, to a separate investigation

28. Von Arnim, *Platos Jugenddialoge*, p. 56.
29. Ibid., pp. 57–59.

from that into love of the Good. Pohlenz was much too quick to identify *endeia* (lack) with *endeia tou agathou* (lack of the Good).[30] At least in his first article, he rushed through the stage where lack is explicitly called "lack of the kindred" (*endeia tou oikeiou*), as distinct from "lack of the Good." In fact, this is the only lack that is ever explicitly mentioned, for when *to oikeion* (the kindred) becomes identified with the Good, *endeia* (lack) has been dropped from the discussion. Thus, von Arnim is correct to charge Pohlenz with failing to see that the desire for completion (*Ergänzung*) through love of the kindred is not necessarily the same as, or even compatible with, the desire for perfection (*Vervollkommnung*) through love of the Good.[31] Even Pohlenz is compelled to admit the possibility that the entire discussion of love of the Good is replaced by a separate one (cf. 221c5–d6). But he argues that this consequence is not established unless the new suggestion is in contradiction to the other.[32] What he ignores, however, is that the entire account of love of the Good is given up as a presupposition for what follows. He thus fails to notice those aspects of this new discussion which are most distinctive.

The "feeling of lack" leads directly to love of one's kindred by nature (*to physei oikeion*, cf. 222a5), and not to love of the Good. This kindred is later identified with the Good only through an abrupt and, to say the least, quite paradoxical turn of the argument. At first, however, Socrates illustrates what "the kindred" is by referring to the friendship between Lysis and Menexenus, who love each other because they are akin to —though not necessarily good for—each other (221e5–6). We

---

30. Pohlenz, book review in *Göttingische gelehrte Anzeigen*, 5:257.
31. Von Arnim, "Platos *Lysis*," pp. 368–369.
32. Pohlenz, "Nochmals Platos *Lysis*," p. 573.

may also observe that Hippothales' feeling of a lack leads him to love Lysis, who is akin to him by virtue of his bashfulness (222b2; cf. 204b5–c2). One can perhaps also say that some lack in Socrates impels him to love and to seek the friendship of Lysis and Menexenus, with whom he has a kind of affinity (223b7). But in none of these cases is it easy to see, without borrowing from Diotima's speech in the *Symposium* or from the *Phaedrus,* how the love of one's kindred leads upward toward the Good. A connection between love of one's kindred by nature and striving for the Good is perhaps suggested if Lysis or Menexenus befriends the "genuine lover" Socrates (222a6–7), out of an awareness of need for the Good. But the other examples are quite different. Neither the friendship between Lysis and Menexenus nor the love affair which Hippothales hopes for with Lysis appears likely to lead beyond itself. The human sense of want seems to aim toward discovery of our natural kin, the avowal of reciprocal love, and a contentment one with the other such as to blunt our awareness of our need for what is good. Were it not for the presence of a Socrates, it seems, human love would quite possibly not lead toward the Good.

Von Arnim, then, is right in arguing that the feeling of lack is not presented as the source, or "real cause," of love of the Good. The notion of *endeia,* in its context in the dialogue, is not a part of the earlier discussion of the Good as friend. This is not to assert, with von Arnim, that the notion is wholly unplatonic. Nor is it to deny that important questions remain about the relationship between the two aspects of friendly love, love of the Good and love of the kindred. How, for example, is the necessarily reciprocal (cf. 222a6–7) love of one's human kindred related to each man's love of the Good? Are even the deepest human attachments merely means in our pursuit of the Good? Or do they spring from some source other than the individual's desire to appropriate for himself what is good? And in this latter case, are these desires of the heart in harmony or in conflict with the desire for the Good?[33] Such questions, however, go beyond the scope of the present discussion. We can not here examine to what extent, and with what transformations, the notion of "the kindred" is preserved in Plato's teaching about friendship. What needs to be emphasized here is merely that *endeia* (lack) is not presented by Plato as the "real cause" of love of the Good.

Since, then, the feeling of lack is not the "real cause" of love of the Good, von Arnim could be right that there is no such cause other than the Good itself. But even if he is mistaken, he is certainly right that this thought, if true, would be a fundamental teaching of the *Lysis*. For in that case, even if all subordinate attachments, including all friendships between men, stemmed in part from our own lacks or our own needs, we could still love the Good for itself alone. Man could escape his poor self by devoting his life to the pursuit of the Good, and to philosophy understood as pursuit of knowledge of the Good. This life would retain its dignity even if its ultimate goal were never completely accessible to man. And if man could become, as von Arnim believes, truly wise and truly good, then the pursuit of this goal would lead to the deepest happiness. According to this interpretation, the *Lysis* reads as an unusually unequivocal recommendation of the Socratic way of life.

One question, however, stands in the way of accepting this

33. "In particular, so long as Plato asked *ti estin to philon,* he had trouble connecting the phenomenon of mutual friendship with the notion of value seen in something cherished." Thomas Gould, *Platonic Love* (New York, 1963), p. 195.

interpretation of true friendly love. Is there indeed *no* "real cause" of love of the Good? Is the Good indeed loved for its own sake? This question leads us back to the question of who it is that loves the Good. For if the Good is loved for its own sake, it would presumably still be loved—even especially so— by those who are themselves good and free of need. This is, of course, a necessary underpinning for von Arnim's separation of *philia* (friendship) from *erōs* (erotic love). But did not Socrates claim that the Good is loved only by imperfect beings, and because of the presence of evils, rather than by those who have already become good? (cf. 218a–b). What happened to the assertions that only intermediates, who are neither good nor bad, love the Good, and that they love it only because of the presence of some evil? Von Arnim is indeed justified in questioning the authority of these statements, since the requirement for the presence of evils as "real cause," and the limitation to intermediates as lovers, are abandoned later in the dialogue. But von Arnim fails to give sufficient thought to the fact, which he of course observes, that the Good as object of love is eliminated at the same time. In other words, he fails to consider that one might not be able to eliminate what is bad as a cause of love without also eliminating the Good as its object. It could be true, however absurd it seems at first, that the Good is a drug (*pharmakon*) against evils and that we would cease to love it if evils were to disappear from the world (220b8–d7). To see how this could be so, let us consider wisdom as an illustration of what the Good might be like. Socrates' first conversation with Lysis recommends philosophy merely as a liberation from the constraints which ignorance places upon our lives. He suggests that if, and only if, Lysis became wise in everything everyone would love him as a friend, and he would be a free man ruling over others. Wisdom or competence is thus presented as a drug against the evils of ignorance and slavery. Later in the dialogue, Socrates broadens this thesis by arguing that only those who are still beset by the evils of ignorance can still love wisdom. Those who already possess wisdom, and who thus are wise, no longer love it (218a2–b3). Indeed, suggests Socrates, no one loves wisdom solely for its own sake, but rather it is loved as a release from the ills of ignorance. And although both Pohlenz and von Arnim regard the thought as thoroughly unplatonic, it is not absurd to suppose that the presence of evils is a necessary condition for love of the Good. How, for example, could we truly love the Good without knowing it to be good? And how could we know that the Good was good without understanding it in the context of life's evils? Would we even become aware that we need to know the Good if we did not suffer repeatedly from our false opinions about it? If there were no evils, present or impending, there might still—as Socrates asserts—be love, friendship, and desire. But these desires would be directed toward what is akin to us, as distinct from what is good.

I conclude, then, that love (or friendship) for the Good would be impossible in a being that was permanently free of wants and needs. Moreover, as I argue in the commentary, this conclusion is compatible with Socrates' restatement at the end of the Lysis (222d6–7) that he who is good is a friend of the Good. And if even our love of the Good is inseparable from our deficiencies, all the more would this be true of love and friendship among human beings. There is no evidence in the Lysis for a kind of possible friendship which is wholly independent of human wants and needs. And Pohlenz was closer than von Arnim to an understanding of Plato's thought about friendship.

Index

Plato's Dialogue on Friendship

Designed by G. T. Whipple, Jr.
Composed by Simpson/Milligan Printing Company, Inc.
in 12 point Compugraphic Bembo, 2 points leaded,
with display lines in Bembo.
Printed offset by Thomson-Shore, Inc.
on Wallen's Number 66 text, 50 pound basis.
Bound by John H. Dekker & Sons, Inc.
in Holliston book cloth
and stamped in All Purpose foil.

Library of Congress Cataloging in Publication Data
(For library cataloging purposes only)
Bolotin, David, 1944-
  Plato's dialogue on friendship.
  Includes bibliographical references and index.
  1. Plato. Lysis.   2. Friendship.   I. Title.
B375.B64   1979   177'.6   79-4041
ISBN   0-8014-1227-7

DATE DUE